DARWIN

Paul Johnson

DARWIN

Portrait of
a Genius

VIKING

VIKING
Published by the Penguin Group
Penguin Group (USA) Inc., 375 Hudson Street,
New York, New York 10014, U.S.A.
Penguin Group (Canada), 90 Eglinton Avenue East, Suite 700, Toronto,
Ontario, Canada M4P 2Y3 (a division of Pearson Penguin Canada Inc.)
Penguin Books Ltd, 80 Strand, London WC2R 0RL, England
Penguin Ireland, 25 St. Stephen's Green, Dublin 2, Ireland
(a division of Penguin Books Ltd)
Penguin Books Australia Ltd, 250 Camberwell Road, Camberwell,
Victoria 3124, Australia (a division of Pearson Australia Group Pty Ltd)
Penguin Books India Pvt Ltd, 11 Community Centre, Panchsheel Park,
New Delhi–110 017, India
Penguin Group (NZ), 67 Apollo Drive, Rosedale, Auckland 0632,
New Zealand (a division of Pearson New Zealand Ltd)
Penguin Books (South Africa) (Pty) Ltd, 24 Sturdee Avenue,
Rosebank, Johannesburg 2196, South Africa

Penguin Books Ltd, Registered Offices: 80 Strand, London WC2R 0RL, England

First published in 2012 by Viking Penguin, a member of Penguin Group (USA) Inc.

1 3 5 7 9 10 8 6 4 2

LIBRARY OF CONGRESS CATALOGING IN PUBLICATION DATA
Johnson, Paul.
Darwin : portrait of a genius / Paul Johnson.
p. cm.
Includes index.
ISBN 978-0-670-02571-8
1. Darwin, Charles, 1809–1882.   2. Naturalists—England—Biography.   I. Title.
QH31.D2J64 2012
576.8'2092—dc23
[B]
2012003433

Printed in the United States of America
Set in Bell MT Std
Designed by Francesca Belanger

ALWAYS LEARNING   PEARSON

To my grandson Ralph

Contents

DARWIN

CHAPTER ONE

A Heritage of Genius, and Its Shadow

A ll his life, Charles Darwin believed that inheritance was much more important in shaping a man or woman than education or environment. Nature rather than nurture was formative, in his view. Though he knew nothing of the science of genetics, and never used the word *gene*, which is first recorded in English in 1911, more than a quarter-century after his death, he is a classic case of genetic inheritance. Indeed, two of his grandparents and his father can reasonably be classified as geniuses.

His paternal grandfather, Erasmus Darwin (1731–1802) came from an old family of modest landowners. After Cambridge, he trained as a doctor in Edinburgh, and then practiced in Litchfield, Dr. Johnson's town (they did not get on). He was successful and had many patients, easily earning £1,000 a year, a handsome income then. News of his skill reached the ears of George III, who invited him to come to London as the royal doctor. But Dr. Darwin declined. The Hanoverian royals were slow at paying their doctors. In any case, Darwin was happy as he was, combining a busy provincial practice with poetry and science. The symbol of this dualism was his coach, which he designed himself. It was fitted up with a writing desk, a skylight, and a portion of his library, so that he could carry on his intellectual pursuits while going on his daily round of professional calls.

His mind was large, noble, and omnivorous. He was interested in every aspect of science, both theoretical and empirical. He had a maxim: "Any man who never conducts an experiment is a fool." He read widely, in French as well as English, and two of his favorite authors were Buffon and Lamarck, both early exponents of the theory of evolution. He met and corresponded with Rousseau. He attended regular discussion groups with early industrialists and inventors, such as Watt and Boulton. His chief passions, however, were botany and animal life. As he prospered, he bought a plot of land and planted an eight-acre experimental garden. He wrote and published a two-part didactic poem, *The Botanic Garden*, covering "The Economy of Vegetation" and "The Loves of the Plants." It was highly successful, much praised by the fastidious Horace Walpole, and translated into French, Italian, and Portuguese. He expanded the lore of his poem in a prose work, *Phytologia; or, The Philosophy of Agriculture and Gardening* (1799), which contains much speculation about the generative life of plants.

However, it is his treatise *Zoonomia; or, The Laws of Organic Life* (1794–96), that best illustrates his imaginative genius. In it he assumed an enormous time span for the earth, a whole generation before Lyall's geological researches established it, and speculated accurately on the successive phases of life that emerged and on its essential unity. He wrote: "As the earth and ocean were probably peopled with vegetable productions long before the existence of animals, and many families of these animals long before other families of them, shall we conjecture that one and the same kind of living filaments is and has been the cause of all organic life?" This was an extraordinarily perceptive question to ask in 1794, and the use of the term *filament* is particularly suggestive, as though he was already intuitively aware of the physical form of the chromosome and capable of leapfrogging over the work of his grandson, Charles Darwin, into the age of genetics.

Erasmus Darwin was an extraordinary polymath, an instinctive inventor of mechanical gadgets, and a man who had theories and ideas about everything. Large and handsome, though also clumsy and accident-prone, he was hugely attractive to women and took full advantage of the fact. Two of his illegitimate children, both clever girls, he set up in a school, and then wrote them a treatise, *A Plan for the Conduct of Female Education in Boarding Schools* (1797), which is full of sound advice, valid today. He was accused of skepticism in his talk, which was jocose, cynical, and "rough." But he wrote:

> Dull atheist, could a giddy dance
> Of atoms lawless hurl'd
> Construct so wonderful, so nice
> So harmonised a world?

Twice married, he had three sons by his first wife. The eldest became a brilliant medical student at Edinburgh but died from an infection received while dissecting. The second was a flourishing solicitor but committed suicide. The third also went to Edinburgh, qualified as a doctor, and practiced at Shrewsbury, becoming in due course one of the wealthiest general practitioners in

England, a man famous in learned circles and a Fellow of the Royal Society. He was also the father of Charles Darwin. By his second wife, Erasmus had four sons and three daughters, one of whom, Violetta, married Tertius Galton and gave birth to Francis Galton, another polymath of genius, who created the science of eugenics.

Whether Erasmus's doctor-son, father of Charles, was a genius is a matter of opinion, but he was certainly remarkable. There seem to be two types of genius, the purely cerebral and the intuitive-cerebral, Galileo being an example of the first and Newton of the second. In his superb essay on Newton, J. M. Keynes, another genius, pointed out that Newton always took a major step forward by an intuitive leap, but then held his discovery tightly by his "strong, intellectual muscle-power," until in due course, satisfied by its veracity, he proceeded to prove it by reason. Darwin's father, Dr. Robert Darwin, was a man of powerful intellect, clearly, but the force of his medical skill arose from his intuitive penetration, which was essentially visual and observational, though aided by the cunning questions he put. One imagines he resembled Dr. Joseph Bell, the famous surgeon, under whom Arthur Conan Doyle worked in Edinburgh and on whom he based his character Sherlock Holmes.

In his autobiographical writings, Charles Darwin gives a striking portrait of his father, dwelling lingeringly, even a little enviously, on his intuitive gifts. Robert Darwin was an immensely hard worker, laboring long hours in his surgery and on his rounds, but he did not seek greatly to enlarge his professional knowledge: His genius lay in immediate, physical contact with the patient, on first diagnosis, on visits, and at every point in the course of the condition. He looked into and through his patients and seems to have inspired in them, almost without exception, a confidence in his capacity to cure them that was nearly miraculous. He was huge, six foot two, and correspondingly big in bone and brawn, "the largest man I ever saw," wrote his son. But his voice was high-pitched. Robert Darwin initially disliked medicine intensely and told his son he would never have practiced it if he could have got an income any other way. But after completing his studies at Leyden, he began to practice while he was only twenty and was an immediate success. His fees during his first year paid for a servant and two horses, and so it continued, with increasing success, for sixty years. He had a particular ability to persuade women to open up and tell him their problems, which were often not so much physical as psychological. He was, in fact, a psychiatrist as well as a physician and was able to charge ten guineas a visit to the many wealthy ladies in the district. Charles Darwin quoted a young doctor as saying that his father was "wholly unscientific" but his "power of predicting the end of an illness was unparalleled." He rightly disapproved of many injurious current practices, such as bleeding—he hated the sight of blood, a horror he passed on to his son—and his treatment was, often enough, sensible advice and reassurance, which, given the state of medical knowledge then, and the unavailability of effective drugs except opium, was just as well. The best doctors in the early nineteenth century were those who, physically, did least, and Robert Darwin was one of them. Instead, he provided wisdom and sensibility.

Erasmus Darwin was a member of the Lunar Society, whose members, the Lunatics, met on moonlit nights when their coachmen could see to drive. They included the Midland intelligentsia and successful businessmen and professionals, chiefly with a scientific bent. Though some might conform to the Church of England for social reasons, nearly all were unorthodox and many were Unitarians. Some were closet skeptics. Among them was Josiah Wedgwood, the Staffordshire potter, and Erasmus succeeded in marrying his doctor son to the potter's eldest child, Susannah. She provided him with six children, the youngest but one being Charles. She was already forty-three when he was born, and when he was eight, she died. Although he described his father in detail, he wrote virtually nothing about his mother, and this chasm in his account of his childhood is significant. We know she was highly intelligent, lively and imaginative, capable of inspiring great affection. But Charles said nothing about his love of her or of his loss. It is a fact that, though fluent and in most ways highly communicative, Charles Darwin never spoke or wrote of the deepest things.

However, he had the Wedgwood genes, and in his maternal grandfather, another genius. There is no doubt about that. Josiah Wedgwood (1730–1795) was the thirteenth and youngest child of an old and highly prolific Midland family, which could trace itself back to the fifteenth century and beyond. Many had been involved in the primitive pottery trade that flourished in northern Staffordshire, especially in Burslem, where Josiah was born. His father died when he was eight, and he was immediately taken from school and put to work. He thus had virtually no education.

But his intelligence was enormous, versatile, highly flexible, and above all, practical. He was an empirical scientist on a superhuman scale. By his early twenties, he was running his own "family" of potbanks, and over the next forty years, he transformed a clumsy handicraft trade into a vast domestic and export industry employing a range of high technologies. He improved every aspect of the business by an endless series of careful and judicious experiments. He introduced uniformity in the plates, so they could be piled without cracking. His teapot lids fitted exactly; his spouts poured gently; his handles could be held without burning the finger. Without any theoretical training or knowledge, he got to understand the physics of baking pots, the chemistry of glazes, dyes, and colors, the geology of clays, and the machinery of mass production. In every department, his changes were fundamental and, eventually, highly successful. Even more remarkable, perhaps, he showed an extraordinary talent for design and a gift for introducing new materials, combinations, and colorings, which gave his pottery, especially the revolutionary Jasperware, an elegance and distinction that led to its worldwide fame. He built an entirely new factory at a place he called Etruria and made it the center of a network of canals and roads. He provided houses and a school, on new and progressive lines. Not least, he showed huge powers of salesmanship and financial acumen so that, when he died, aged sixty-four, he left to his heirs an immense business plus half a million pounds in cash.

As the progeny of three such remarkable men, Eramus and Robert Darwin and Josiah Wedgwood—the imaginative genius, the intuitive genius, and the empirical genius—Charles Darwin had access to a gene pool of the highest possible quality. Some points are worth noting. First, all three forebears were skillful at handling money and amassed it with the seemingly effortless ease that financial wizards show. Hence Charles Darwin was able to become a gentleman-scientist without the smallest difficulty and remain one all his life. He never had to worry about money. He *did* worry about money—he worried about everything—but he never had to compromise, limit, or adjust his scientific activities for financial reasons. Thus he was virtually unique among famous scientists. Moreover, he inherited the talent for managing money, unlike his codiscoverer and rival, Alfred Russel Wallace, who came from a family of financial bunglers and bankrupts and got into a mess in his turn, from which Darwin rescued him. Not that the Darwins and Wedgwoods were all wizards with coin: Both families had their share of personal boom-and-busters (Charles's solicitor uncle was one). But Charles Darwin, though he never earned a penny in salary and made scarcely £10,000 from his books in his lifetime, grew steadily richer, and in his last years had an investment income alone of over £8,000 a year, leaving at his death a fortune of "at least" £280,000. (By comparison, Dickens, for all his bestsellers and spectacular readings, left just under £90,000. Palmerston, over fifty years in well-paid office, with successful investments in land, slateworks, and a port, left under £100,000.)

The Darwin and Wedgwood families were thus favored by wealth makers and preservers, as well as spendthrifts. They were highly philoprogenitive and clustered in great family groups, living nearby and thus often intermarrying. Charles Darwin conformed to genotype in both respects, marrying his first cousin and begetting ten children, seven of whom survived to maturity. There were a number of tragic cases among the Darwin-Wedgwood cousinhoods. Erasmus Darwin's first wife, Charles Darwin's paternal grandmother, took to drinking gin and died an alcoholic, by no means unusual among wealthy English ladies in the second half of the eighteenth century, as Thomas Rowlandson suggests with his superb watercolor, *The Morning Dram.* She was not the only drunk in the clan, and there were cases of drug addiction, too (opium), also common enough, especially in the years 1800–1850. And there were several suicides.

In general, however, the family confederation did well and populated the Midlands and the south of England with well-to-do families of professionals and businessmen, who kept in touch and made their own networks of friends. Charles Darwin was thus born into a teeming and valuable acquaintance, which he assiduously maintained and polished all his life, in many different ways but especially by a vast correspondence. Its characteristics were high intelligence, an interest in technical and scientific matters, religious unorthodoxy or disbelief, industry, and persistence. Fellows of the Royal Society and fellows of the Geographical, Geological, Botanical, and other learned societies were common. Acquisitiveness, not just in money and property, but in specimens of every kind, from butterflies to fossils, was almost universal, and the comfortable rectories and purpose-built villas in which the families lived were crammed with books and cases of stuffed birds and animals, rocks and potsherds, their spacious gardens often containing ranks of specimen trees and exotic shrubs.

Gardens, servants of all kinds, and children of all ages abounded. Darwin conformed to this pattern in every respect, during all his mortal existence.

There was one shadow, however. Among Erasmus Darwin's friends was Joseph Priestley, minister and theologian variously described as an Arminian, Socinian, and an atheist but chiefly remarkable for his work as an experimental chemist, as the discoverer of oxygen. From time to time, writings of his were publicly burned, but he was generally left alone until the coming of the French Revolution raised political passions. He foolishly described his political *Letters*, published in 1790, as "grains of Gunpowder" for which his opponents were "providing the match." Hence he was called Gunpowder Priestley. It was an age of "constitutional societies," formed to support the French Revolution and press for similar reforms in England, and also of Church-and-King organizations to oppose them. On July 14, 1791, Priestley was invited to address a meeting in Birmingham to commemorate the anniversary of the Fall of the Bastille, but having been warned of danger, he declined to attend. Even so, a Church-and-King mob surrounded his house at Fairhill, near Birmingham, and burned it, destroying nearly all his books, scientific apparatus, and papers. Priestley escaped with his life, but order was not restored for three days. Four rioters were hanged, Priestley received some compensation, and friends enabled him to resettle in London. But he never felt safe again, and in 1794 he emigrated to New York. The victimization and enforced exile of Priestley became a defining event in the Darwin family, and among all their dissenting and unorthodox friends. Charles Darwin was vividly conscious of it, more so indeed than his grandfather and father. What terrified him was the religious dimension of the event. It left him with an abiding fear of the possible consequences of offending the tender consciences of Church of England clergymen, who might then be inspired to stir up a mob to burn and kill. The cry of the mob, who were said to have called out "No philosophers—Church and King for ever!" and "Burn the atheists!" always echoed in his subconscious and preyed on his nerves. It gave to his life and work a dimension of worry that had enormous consequences.

CHAPTER TWO

Education and Self-Education of a Scientist

Charles Darwin was born on February 12, 1809, at The Mount, Shrewsbury, the substantial house his father had built in the early Regency style. It was a vintage year for great men: Also born were Tennyson and Gladstone, and Lincoln arrived the same day as Darwin. Napoléon still strode over Europe like a colossus, and Madison was about to be inaugurated as the fourth president of the United States. But the item from 1809 that would most have interested the adult Darwin was the news that a young naturalist and artist, John James Audubon, had successfully banded pewees near Pittsburgh, proving that migratory birds return to nest to the place where they hatched. This was the kind of experiment dear to Darwin's heart, and he would have endorsed Audubon's remarks when he first saw a ringed female pewee lay an egg: "It filled my mind with the same wonder that I feel when I search the heavens for the meaning of all I see."

Throughout his long life, Darwin was an extremely lucky man. Of all the great scientists in history, he was the most favored by fortune. His genetic inheritance, as we have seen, was magnificent. He had a happy childhood, despite the catastrophe of his mother's death. He loved and admired his father. He was happy in his father's house, garden, and fields. The family was harmonious and the servants plentiful, well paid, and friendly. Darwin was born a gentleman in an age when the term had a specific meaning and legal status. His uncle, Josiah Wedgwood II, had bought a prize thousand-acre estate at Maer in Staffordshire, and there Darwin often stayed in childhood and youth, and learned to ride and shoot. Under the game laws, then strict and fiercely enforced, you had to be "qualified" to shoot game. Darwin was, by virtue of his father's ownership of land. He wrote: "I became passionately fond of shooting & I do not believe that anyone could have shown more zeal for the most holy cause than I did for shooting birds." He remembered "killing my first snipe, & my excitement was so great that I had much difficulty in reloading my gun from the trembling of my hands." He became "a very good shot." At one point, his zeal for shooting became such that his father angrily remarked it was the only thing he cared about. This was not true. Shooting revealed the ambiguity that was one of Darwin's most marked characteristics. He regarded it as an intellectual activity: "It required so much skill to judge where to find most game & hunt the dogs well." It also taught him the importance of records: "I kept an exact record of every bird that I shot." Moreover, from reading Gilbert White's *The Natural History and Antiquities of Selborne*, he "took much pleasure in watching the habits of birds & even made notes on the subject." He wondered "why every gentleman did not become an ornithologist." Thus sport nurtured science, and Darwin saw no conflict. Though he gave up shooting for pleasure in his early forties, at no point did he find it anomalous to hunt, catch, kill, and dissect enormous numbers of insects, invertebrates, birds, and animals in the quest for knowledge, despite detesting cruelty in any form and acquiring a positive affection for many of the species he investigated.

Darwin seems to have been a collector from a very early age: "shells, seals, franks, coins & minerals." He wrote that it is this "passion for collecting" that leads "a man to become a systematic naturalist," and in his case "was clearly innate as none of my sisters or brother ever had this taste." His first serious collection was of beetles, and "to give a proof of my zeal," he one day "saw two rare beetles & seized one in each hand; then I saw a third & new kind, which I could not bear to lose, so that I popped the one I held in my right hand into my mouth. Alas it ejected some intensely acrid fluid which burnt my tongue so that I was forced to spit the beetle out, which was lost."

It was Darwin's strategy, in writing about himself after he became famous, to emphasize the positive side of his intellectual development as springing from innate qualities and to discount his formal education. He had a year at a primary school before going to Shrewsbury for five years. This ancient school, which in Tudor and early Stuart times had been the best in England, was then run by Dr. Samuel Butler. His grandson, another Samuel, was later to hound Darwin unmercifully in his years of fame, and perhaps for this reason, Darwin claimed he learned nothing of value at his grandfather's school. This was not true. He acquired a better command of written English than is the fate of most scientists, together with habits of industry and intellectual tidiness. He also developed a strong taste for literature, especially poetry and, not least, Shakespeare, and the recent poems of Scott and Byron. He made many friends among the boys, and he displayed for the first time a gift that he retained all his life, for male friendship. He said, "Some of these boys were rather clever," but, he added with a hint of satisfaction, "not one of them became in the least distinguished."

Considering Dr. Robert Darwin's skill in judging character and intuiting the thoughts of his patients, it is odd that he had no success at all in picking the right training for his son Charles. He first sent him to Edinburgh to qualify as a doctor like himself. Then, after two full sessions, he switched him to Cambridge (Christ's College) to prepare for ordination. Charles never showed the slightest enthusiasm or aptitude for medical or clerical life. Quite the contrary, in both cases. Still, these were two of the best universities in the world, and Darwin had the means to take the fullest advantage of their opportunities. His father always provided him with plenty of money. Thus, for his beetle hobby, he was able to employ a man in the winter to scrape the moss off old trees and bag it, and to collect rubbish from the hulls of barges from the fens: "Thus I got some very rare species." Still, he missed a number of chances. In the Edinburgh medical school, he allowed his squeamishness to inhibit his study of dissection, and he never learned the basic scientific principles of it or acquired the dexterity common in expert surgeons. As he spent much of his later life dissecting, this was a serious omission. In addition, he never learned human anatomy. Hatred of this essential but dull, difficult, and exhausting business is the biggest single reason why medical students give up or fail their course, today as then. So Darwin's omission was not surprising. Nevertheless, ignorance of anatomy was always a handicap in his career. Indeed, his failure at Edinburgh to learn more about the human body was the reason why, as a student of organic life, he was always stronger on flora and fauna than on people. He became a consummate scientific polymath in many ways, but anthropology was his weak subject, and this helps to explain why the *Origin of Species* is so much better a book than *The Descent of Man*, and why Darwin came, in effect, almost to a full stop at the height of his career.

Darwin also failed to acquire, as he admits, any skill in drawing, though there were plenty of opportunities, and this made it difficult later for him to produce effective diagrams in his works or visual illustrations to organize parts hard to describe in words. He also admits he failed to compensate by hard study for his natural lack of aptitude in modern languages. This meant he never acquired the habit of automatically reading scientific publications except in English, and it is one reason why he failed to spot Gregor Mendel's key paper on genetics in 1866 (to be sure, so did most other people). Darwin, thanks to private tuition, mastered Euclid, and he exulted in the pleasure he got from becoming familiar with the process of logical proof. More seriously, however, he failed very largely to progress in mathematics beyond the elementary stages, and this cost him dear. As Galileo observed:

The universe cannot be read until we have learned the language and have become familiar with the characters in which it has been written. It is written in mathematical language, and the letters are triangles, circles and other mathematical figures, without which means it is humanly impossible to comprehend a single word.

It may be said that Darwin was not seeking to comprehend the universe as a whole, but only its organic content. But even there the mathematical aspects were to be recognized as vital in the generation after Darwin's death. As Francis Crick, who built so strikingly on Darwin's foundation, was to put it, in *What Mad Pursuit* (1988): "Almost all aspects of [organic] life are engineered at the molecular level, and without understanding molecules we can have only a very sketchy understanding of life itself."

If Darwin had understood and used mathematics, he might have penetrated to the molecular level and to the genetic dimension that completed his discoveries—and also avoided some serious errors of comprehension, as we shall see. His lack of math, which he shared with his codiscoverer of natural selection, Wallace, was his most serious educational handicap.

Nevertheless, Darwin's time at Edinburgh and Cambridge was of inestimable value to him, especially at a personal level. It was full of memorable incidents, as when at Edinburgh he attended a meeting of the Royal Society presided over by Sir Walter Scott, or in Cambridge where he saw two body snatchers lynched by a mob, a grisly scene that reinforced the "Priestley fear" in his subconscious. There was one academic exercise in particular that proved invaluable. To get his BA degree at Cambridge, he was obliged to read thoroughly William Paley's *View of the Evidences of Christianity*. This work was and still is remarkable not so much because it "proves" that nature is the work of a

Supreme Being but because it is a model of deductive logic, step-by-step argument, and not least, clarity of exposition. There is no doubt at all that Darwin learned a great deal from Paley about how exactly to put a lucid, cogent, and sustained case, and that if he had not read and absorbed it, *The Origin of Species* would have been a much less effective book.

Finally, and most important, these sojourns in high places of learning were vital because of the scholars he met and the relationships he formed with them. It is not considered quite proper to suggest that scientists often progress as much by personal charm as by intellect. But it is so. Darwin is an example. Within the limits he set himself, he was gregarious, and there is overwhelming evidence that people liked him and took to him. He could attract, interest, and above all, charm, when he wished to do so. Moreover, he enjoyed working among the learned at a professional level. He had a natural gift for what we now call networking, and a taste for it too. Edinburgh and Cambridge gave him the opportunity to lay the foundation of an immense range of contacts in the scientific world, and he took full advantage of it.

These included, at Edinburgh, the professor of chemistry, Thomas Hope, and Robert Jameson, professor of natural history. Jameson had founded the Plinean Society, to which students could belong and contribute, and there Darwin delivered his first scientific paper, on the sea mat *Flustra*, a primitive creature rather like a piece of moss. He also belonged to the Wernerian Natural History Society and took an active part in it. At such bodies, he made friends with the marine biologist Dr. Robert Edmund Grant, the biologist Dr. John Coldstream, and the polymath William Gregory, later a famous scientific writer, all of whom proved useful in due course. In pursuit of *Flustra*, he went with members of both bodies on scientific expeditions along the eastern Scottish coast. He learned taxidermy from John Edmonstone, a freed slave who had been trained by the famous traveler-naturalist Charles "Squire" Waterton. He heard Audubon lecture on birds. He spent a winter with Robert Edmond Grant, who had taken a house on the Prestonpans shore to study sponges and polyps, and helped him produce a score of scientific papers published in the late 1820s. He filled the first of his mature scientific notebooks. He studied Lamarck assiduously, especially his *System of Invertebrate Animals*, and became a convert to his system of evolution. The atmosphere at Edinburgh was radical, often wildly so, skeptical, nonconformist, innovative, and challenging of all orthodoxies, and Darwin, in his quiet way, absorbed it fully. The impression he later gave that he wasted his time at medical school was false. He learned a great deal, as well as making scores of contacts.

Darwin's years at Cambridge were in some ways even more fruitful. Darwin lived well—he could afford, for instance, to pay the boy choristers of King's College Chapel to sing in his rooms at parties for his friends—and he entertained the scientific dons. Among them was the Reverend Adam Sedgwick, professor of geology, whose superb lectures he attended and whom he was privileged to accompany on a scientific expedition to the Welsh mountains, where he learned the invaluable techniques of spotting rock strata and taking samples. Even more important was the Reverend John Stevens Henslow, formerly professor of mineralogy, now professor of botany and a general scientific polymath.

Darwin cultivated him assiduously, and he became in turn devoted to the young man. Darwin said he "took long walks with him most days," so he was known to the dons as "the man who walks with Henslow." Darwin said Henslow's "strongest taste was to draw conclusions from long continued minute observations," something Darwin learned to emulate. He learned much else about a wide range of scientific disciplines, including the need to take systematic and copious notes. His "intimacy" with Henslow, Darwin wrote, "was an inestimable benefit."

Moreover, Henslow had wide contacts and used them to favor students he esteemed. At the end of the summer of 1831, he wrote to Darwin saying he had been asked to recommend a young gentleman naturalist to accompany a global voyage by a naval ten-gun brig for scientific purposes. "You are the very man they are in search of." Darwin, we have noted, was an exceptionally lucky man. This was the biggest stroke of luck of his entire life. Yet it was not just luck. The First Reform Bill was then before Parliament, and the old order was changing. But in 1831, it was still largely intact, and plum appointments went by privileged contacts. Robert FitzRoy, captain of the HMS *Beagle*, was himself an aristocrat, pushed up to captain at the early age of twenty-seven and now given this excellent assignment, largely because his uncle had been Viscount Castlereagh, the famous foreign secretary. But it was a lonely job, for as captain and commander, he had powers of life and death over the crew and necessarily kept aloof from them. On a long voyage—this was planned for two years and actually took nearly five—such isolation could be fatal, and FitzRoy's predecessor had committed suicide. What the captain wanted, as his naturalist, was a *gentleman* companion, with the stress on gentleman, who could share his day cabin and his table. Darwin, as Henslow noted, was "not a *finished* naturalist," but well on the way: almost certainly the best-educated student naturalist then at Cambridge. But more important, he had the manners and means of a gentleman. His father supplied him with ample funds, which enabled him to hire Syms Covington as a valet-assistant at £60 a year (then a huge salary for a servant) and to ensure that all his specimens and notes were periodically sent back to England during the long voyage by the safest and most expeditious route. The FitzRoy-Darwin combination was thus a double job, as was underlined by the original ship's doctor, who expected to act as naturalist, but who discharged himself as soon as the *Beagle* touched port in South America, disgusted with the setup. But the arrangement worked perfectly. FitzRoy was a man with an incandescent temper who occasionally stormed at his companion (he eventually blew his own brains out), but he was an excellent navigator, quickly saw the point of Darwin, and fitted the ship's movements to his program of work. Darwin, for his part, was quiet, obsequious, and conciliatory.

Darwin was given only a month to prepare for his voyage. The *Beagle* left Devonport on December 27, 1831, and returned to England on October 2, 1836. It visited the Cape Verde Islands, various places in Brazil and Argentina, including Rio de Janeiro and Buenos Aires, the Falkland Islands, Patagonia, Tierra del Fuego, the Straits of Magellan, Central Chile, Chiloé and the Chonos Islands, the extreme earthquake region of Chile at Valdivia, northern Chile and Peru, the Galápagos Archipelago, Tahiti, New

Zealand, Australia, the coral formations of Keeling Island, and Mauritius. At intervals in the five-year voyage, Darwin was able to spend a total of three years and one month on land, traveling widely, collecting botanical, organic, animal, fossil, metallurgical, and mineral specimens of all kinds and recording his observations of flora, fauna, and human inhabitants. He shot a wide variety of birds and animals, went on an ostrich hunt, studied the effects of a large-scale earthquake, observed a major volcanic eruption, and visited at length tropical rain forests, high mountains, sierras, pampas and other grasslands, rivers, lakes, and a wide variety of scrub and brushwood areas, as well as scores of native villages, settler towns, mines, and cities.

Apart from his older contemporary, the great German naturalist Alexander von Humboldt, who spent the years 1799–1804 in Latin America, no other scientist had traveled anything like so long as Darwin making studies on the spot or had observed so wide a variety of phenomena on land and ocean. He rightly called the voyage "the most important event of my life." The extensive records he kept, both descriptive and speculative, and the specimens he shipped home and brought back with him provided material on which he worked and published, over the next twenty years and which influenced his thinking over the entire range of his activities for the rest of his life. He wrote a comprehensive account, *Journal of Researches into the Natural History and Geology of the Countries Visited during the voyage of HMS* Beagle *round the World, under the Command of Captain FitzRoy RN*, which formed the first volume of the three-volume report presented by FitzRoy to the admiralty and was later revised and republished as *The*

Voyage of the Beagle. In addition, Darwin produced and printed a large number of learned articles and three books arising from the voyage. He also circulated his observations, discoveries, and notes widely among the scientific community during the voyage, so that by the time he returned, he was already becoming well known and highly respected among his peers, and this esteem was reinforced by his publications. By 1840, when he was in his early thirties, he was on the edge of fame.

It is important to grasp that Darwin was not only a cerebral and intuitive man but a highly emotional one. He received a number of shocks on the voyage that permanently altered the way he saw things. The first concerned the variety of human beings and those he termed "savages." On the *Beagle* were two men and a woman, Yahgan Indians, natives of Tierra del Fuego, who had been picked up on an earlier voyage, taken to England and "civilized," and were now being returned. One of them, called Jemmy Button, had been extremely kind to Darwin when he suffered dreadfully from seasickness in the first week of the voyage. The three did not prepare Darwin for what he saw as the "horrible experience" of meeting Yahgans in their pristine state when the ship touched land in Tierra del Fuego. He wrote: "I could not have believed how wide was the difference between savage and civilized man: it is greater than between a wild and domesticated animal, inasmuch as in a man there is a greater power of improvement." Darwin was astounded by what he thought was the misery, cruelty, aimlessness, and primitive nullity of the Fuegans' lives. He came to believe they were cannibals, constantly engaged in vicious and murderous warfare with other tribes, their neighbors, and even with their own families, virtually devoid of religious or moral beliefs or instincts, without any kind of culture, and not only illiterate but also inarticulate.

We come here to a characteristic of Darwin that must be seen as a serious weakness in his equipment as a scientist. He was a poor anthropologist. He did not bring to his observation of humans the same care, objectivity, acute notation, and calmness he always showed when studying birds and sea creatures, insects, plants, and animals. He jumped to hasty conclusions and believed gossip (in this case from the *Beagle*'s sailors). Almost everything he wrote or believed about the Fuegans was quite untrue. They were not cannibals. They had a horror of eating human flesh. They were kindly and altruistic, especially within the family and tribe. They were little inclined to violence. They had a good deal of culture, an elaborate religion, and many skills and aptitudes. A missionary, Thomas Bridges, settled among them some years after Darwin's visit and compiled a dictionary of their languages, which contained 32,000 words but is incomplete. His son, Lucas Bridges, was born there and wrote an account of the savages that contradicts Darwin at every point. The Fuegans were not the only "savages" Darwin misunderstood as a result of superficial observation and mistaken conclusions. He grossly underrated the Maoris of New Zealand, contrasting them with the Tahitians. "One glance at their respective expressions," he wrote, "brings conviction to the mind that one is a savage, the other a civilized man." The Maoris were guilty of "cunning and ferocity," their houses and persons were "filthily dirty and offensive," and "the idea of washing" never "seems to have entered their heads." Fascinated by facial expressions, from which he deduced all kinds of scientific conclusions, Darwin noted, as a sign of savagery, the "air of rigid inflexibility" of the Maori expressions. His picture of the Maoris rivals the inaccuracy of his attack on the Fuegans, but it was the Fuegan experience that did permanent damage to Darwin as a scientist, for the emotional shock, which came to him as a crucial revelation, led him for the first time to see the evolution of savage to civilized man as a fearful struggle to break out of endless cycles of cruelty and killing in a desperate effort to survive—what Thomas Hobbes called "the war of everyman against everyman." His experience in Tierra del Fuego was of paramount importance in persuading Darwin to see evolution as a theater of violence.

The second shock Darwin experienced on the *Beagle* was the emotional frisson of grasping the immensity of time. He became aware of the colossal age of the universe and the earth within it, of the time-space available for almost unimaginable numbers of minute changes to take place and cumulatively to effect stagger-ing transformations. The year before the *Beagle* set out, Charles Lyell (1797–1875), the great geologist, had published the first vol-ume of his three-volume work, *The Principles of Geology* (subse-quent volumes came out in 1832 and 1833). Captain FitzRoy, who kept up with the latest scientific publications, presented Darwin with the book before they set out, and he read it, was enthralled, and got the other two volumes later in the voyage. Lyell demon-strated, beyond any possibility of doubt, that by dividing the geo-logical system into three groups, which he called by the names still used, Eocene, Miocene, and Pliocene, characterized by the proportion of recent to extinct species of shells embedded in the rocks, the age of the earth could be calculated in many millions of years instead of the total of about six thousand reached by extrapolating figures given in Genesis and other biblical records. Belief in the literal accuracy of the Old Testament had been declining sharply among the educated since the late eighteenth century, but Lyell's work, which was very comprehensive, serious, and persuasive, quite devoid of any antireligious animus, made it quite impossible to accept the Bible any longer as a guide to the chronology of creation. Though Lyell remained a believing Christian and a regular communicant in the Church of England to his death in 1875, his work was more effective in presenting the scientific case against biblical fundamentalism than anything that followed, including Darwin's own *Origin of Species*. Its effect on Darwin was not so much to destroy his faith as to open up possibilities. There was no need to look for catastrophic events and huge shocks in bringing about the world we knew and the organic creatures and vegetation on it and beneath its oceans. There had been plenty of time for everything in creation to emerge gradually, as Darwin had already observed nature tended to operate, so gradually that natural progress could be described as an endless succession of minute events rather than bold acts of creation.

Toward the end of the *Beagle*'s voyage, in the spring of 1836, he had a first-class opportunity of observing such a process of infinite minutiae when the ship called at the Cocos or Keeling Islands in the Indian Ocean. For the purpose of compiling a global record of navigable harbors, the Admiralty had ordered FitzRoy to investigate how ocean coral reefs were formed, to create anchorages. Darwin was put in charge of the project, and he conducted it with such thoroughness and success as to give complete satisfaction to FitzRoy, the Admiralty, and not least, to himself. This particular project, studying the way in which nature effects major changes by a series of countless minute changes over long periods, was exactly to his taste and appealed strongly to Darwin's particular kind of intellect. He much preferred the tiny to the gigantic and the slow to the sudden. The formation of oceanic reefs and atolls from coral polyps had been going on for eons, and the results were measurable. But it was still going on, and human memory was available to record recent results. The formation was not gradual only, for earthquakes and major storms hastened, reinforced, or diverted the process, and by questioning sailors, missionaries, and natives, Darwin was able to include this kind of evidence. But his chief interest was in the actual coral formation, its accumulation, the subsistence it provided, and its relationship to volcanoes, active or dormant, and to areas where the earth's crust was pushing up or settling down. He was able to divide coral reefs and atolls into distinct categories, explaining why differences occurred, and to show why they occurred in specific parts of the sea, such as the South Pacific and Indian Oceans, and not in others, such as the Caribbean. He supplied various diagrams of coral formations, and when his material, expanded from his account in the *Beagle* voyage, was eventually published in book form, he produced a world map, too. But he clearly wrote about coral with great pleasure, certitude, and the admirable clarity and logic he had learned from Paley, and so produced the best thing he had written so far, and the best science.

The year before, however, he had made observations and

discoveries that in the long run were to have an even more profound effect on his knowledge of natural processes, his thinking,
and his great work. Off the coast of Chile, so far off as to be sel-
dom visited, the *Beagle* anchored in the Galápagos, a group of ten
islands, and numerous rocky islets of volcanic formation. Darwin
took intense delight in investigating the creatures he found there,
including giant tortoises, marine and terrestrial lizards, and
numerous birds, especially finches. It was easy for the *Beagle* to
dump him and a colleague, plus servants, on an island for a week
at a time, while it went off to take aboard fresh water supplies. So
Darwin had a good chance to make detailed observations, while
living off "excellent" turtle soup and the "very good" roasted
breastplate of young turtles. He examined the birds in particular,
especially the twenty-six kinds of land birds. He was intrigued by
"a most singular group of finches," thirteen species, divided into
four subgroups. He noted that all the species were peculiar to the
Galápagos, with but one exception, and that there were small but
significant variations in their beaks. He did drawings of them and
then added a significant sentence: "Seeing this gradation and
diversity of structure in one small, intimately related group of
birds, one might really fancy that from an original paucity of
birds in this archipelago, one species had been taken and modi-
fied for different ends." Here was the germ of a seminal idea. He
investigated many other creatures—waders, owls, doves, gulls,
reptiles (especially the tortoises and lizards, dissecting a number,
opening their stomachs and examining the contents), fifteen
kinds of sea fish, and insects—and went thoroughly into the botany of the islands. It is characteristic of his industry that he

recorded 225 species of flowering plants, 100 of them not noted before, and that he sent home 193 specimens of them.

What particularly struck Darwin, and the shock was again emotional as well as cerebral, was the distinctiveness of the flora and fauna of the island group. Though they were five hundred to six hundred miles from the mainland, driftwood, bamboo, and other objects from South America often washed up on the islands, and the Galápagos were clearly part of the continent zoologically and in other ways. But "we see that a vast majority of all the land animals, and that more than half of the flowering plants, are aboriginal productions." He also found "by far the most remarkable feature in the natural history of the archipelago" was that "the different islands to a considerable extent are inhabited by a different set of beings." He was in the islands just long enough to observe the fact. The locals, he found, could look at creatures or plants and tell you which island they came from. In short, not only had organisms on the islands evolved differently from the mainland, but within the group, distinct evolutions or transformations were taking place. Here indeed was food for thought. "We seem," Darwin wrote, "to be brought near to that great fact—the mystery of mysteries—the first appearance of new beings on this earth."

The *Beagle* voyage transformed Darwin from a promising naturalist to a widely experienced and dedicated one. He now knew what he loved: to investigate nature in the greatest possible detail and on the widest possible scale. He said later that he had become a machine for accumulating countless facts and finding out from them universal laws. He delighted in being that machine.

His father, impressed by what had been done on the voyage and gratified that his son was already becoming known in learned circles as a hard worker and a man on the way up, also noticed a physical change: the shape of his head was different. Coming from a doctor as sharp as Robert Darwin, this is worth recording. Maturity had occurred. At this time, Darwin became pleasurably aware that his father now plainly had the intention, and had the means, to set up his son as a gentleman-scientist, free from financial worries and able to devote his entire time to research. It is important to grasp the point: Darwin never had to exhaust his energies on teaching, to scrabble about to get an academic appointment, or to keep it by conforming to the fashions and prejudices of the academy and its rules about publication. This had disadvantages, as we shall see. But the overwhelming advantage was to give the twenty-seven-year-old complete freedom to pursue lines of inquiry he thought most likely to produce worthwhile knowledge, especially about "the mystery of mysteries," for as long as they might require. He had no one to report to except his own conscience and no institution or body to fit in with except the confraternity of learned men. Was ever a scientist more fortunate or more happy?

CHAPTER THREE

The Loss of God

D arwin returned to England in 1836, landing at Falmouth on October 2. He told his uncle Josiah Wedgwood, "I am so happy I hardly know what I am writing." He quickly began networking, oscillating between Cambridge, where he reestablished close relations with Henslow and Sedgwick, and London, especially the Geological and Zoological societies, the Royal Society, the British Museum, and London University, in all of which he found himself an established authority, "a universal collector," in the words of another leisured naturalist, Charles Bunbury, who had identified new species "to the surprise of the big wigs." The first major contact Darwin made, on October 29, was with the great Lyell himself. They instantly became friends and allies and remained so for the rest of their lives. He had a huge haul of specimens, unpacked from the *Beagle* by his valet-assistant, Covington; these served as working capital in ingratiating himself with the experts and institutions among which he divided them. His fossil mammals were regarded as the greatest treasures and brought him the most acclaim.

From the winter of 1836, Darwin can be regarded as a fixture in English savant society, a celebrity. First he lodged in Fitzwilliam Street, Cambridge, then moved into the same street as his brother Erasmus in London. He was elected to the Geological Society as a fellow, and two years later, having presented 80 mammals and 450 birds, to a similar fellowship at the Zoological Society. He led a busy and purposeful social life, getting to know such useful celebrities as the journalist Harriet Martineau, the first great female economist, who was capable of pushing any theory or cause she believed in with tremendous force. He attended the regular Saturday parties of the mathematical inventor Charles Babbage, who designed and constructed the first working computer and who attracted to his Mayfair entertainments the scientific and scholarly elite.

While socializing at night, Darwin was busy by day garnering the results of his five years on the *Beagle*. On January 4, 1837, he read to the Geological Society his first mature scientific paper, on the way in which the western coast of South America had been thrust upward. It was so well received that he said he "felt like a peacock admiring his tail." This was the first of many papers produced for half a dozen learned bodies over the next decade. He was also busy editing *The Zoology of HMS* Beagle, to which famous figures like Richard Owen, John Gould, Thomas Bell, and others contributed, and producing monographs of his own, such as "Observations on the Parallel Roads of Glen Roy," published in the prestigious *Philosophical Transactions of the Royal Society*, his atoll book *The Structure and Distribution of Coral Reefs*, published in 1842, and *Geological Observations on the Volcanic Islands Visited during the Voyage of HMS* Beagle (1844), as well as the *Journal of Researches*, which went into a revised edition in 1845 published by the leading London publisher, John Murray, in his famous Colonial and Home Library. Thus the first major chunk of his published scientific work, eventually to encompass fifteen substantial volumes, reached the public.

But Darwin was also working hard on new material, involving plants and birds and mammals of all kinds, and keeping private notebooks relating to "man, mind and materialism," as he put it, and especially to the way in which species evolved or, as he preferred to put it, were "transmuted." These notebooks housed the raw materials, in thoughts and facts, from which his masterpiece, *The Origin of Species,* was to emerge. He was also voraciously reading scientific publications, as well as books on a wide variety of subjects. In 1838 he came across the sixth edition of a famous book, Thomas Malthus's *Essay on Population,* originally published in 1798. This had a huge emotional impact on him, equivalent to the ones he had felt when he first experienced the savages of Tierra del Fuego, investigated the species of the Galápagos Islands, or examined the coral reefs of the Indian Ocean. An entry in his notebook on September 28, 1838, reveals him shattered and excited by reading Malthus's text and considering its implications for his work.

Ever since he became a systematic naturalist, Darwin had been an evolutionist. That is, he dismissed the account in Genesis of the separate creation of species by Yahweh as symbolic and not to be taken literally. They had, in some way, evolved. There was nothing new, surprising, or alarming in this view. His grandfather had been an evolutionist. So had his French mentors, Buffon and Lamarck. So had other, more distant, thinkers. It was arguable that Francis Bacon had posited some form of evolution, and even that it went back to the pre-Socratic Greeks. Moreover, by the late 1830s, evolution, as opposed to revolution, was a commonplace of philosophers, political and economic, as a natural and desirable way of proceeding in the development of institutions, societies, and much else. The German philosophical heavyweights, Kant and, still more, Hegel, had shown evolution to be inherent in many disciplines and in religion itself. Art, architecture, music, and literature evolved. The English constitution, seen as perfect by many Englishmen and widely admired all over the world, was regarded as a model instance of evolution. The principle was constantly invoked by Goethe. The word comes from classical times and denotes the motion of unrolling a scroll. As set out in Buffon's evolutionary theory of 1762, what happens in nature is that the embryo or germ, instead of being brought into existence by the process of fecundation, is a development or expansion of a preexisting form, which contains the rudiments of all the parts of the future organism.

By the early 1830s, evolution was rapidly becoming the consensus of scientists studying organic life. The term was first used, or rather emphasized, in a heavyweight publication in Lyell's *Principles of Geology*, when he insisted that "the testacea [shellfish] of the ocean existed first, until some of them, by gradual evolution, were improved into those inhabiting the land." Darwin, on his *Beagle* travels, encountered innumerable examples of evolution at all levels, including the highest—hence his emotional belief that the gap between savages and civilized men was greater than that between wild and domesticated animals. He saw, in short, that evolution *had* occurred. What he wanted to discover was *why* it had occurred, as a prelude to finding out *how* it had occurred.

Darwin never got to the latter question because, as we shall see, he missed a vital trick in the game he was playing. But reading Malthus, he concluded, gave him the answer to *why:* Species evolved because they had to, to survive at all. He read it in what, from his account, was a state of emotional fervor. It tied in exactly with his feelings on first seeing the "savages" of Tierra del Fuego. Life was a ferocious struggle not only between species but within them. This was because the fecundity of production in life forms greatly exceeded any increase in their food supplies. And the struggle itself was the engine of evolution, for it meant that only those forms whose variations gave them an edge over their competitors survived, and the process produced not only improved species but also new ones. The phenomenon was not wholly unlike the coral accumulation, which raised atolls and reefs, and it certainly tied in with the variations and developments of finches' beaks in the Galápagos. For the first time Darwin was able to come to a grand conclusion that united the thrusts of his most exciting discoveries during the *Beagle* voyage and turned their dynamic power into a mighty engine of scientific explanation. The process of creation that the Bible attributed to God was not necessary because nature did it herself. By a process of selection over countless generations, nature pushed forward those creatures best able to compete, in countless different and often forceful, cruel, and savage ways, for the available food supplies. There was no controlling spirit: The process was autonomous. There was no designer. The improved forms were the result of automatic selection over innumerable generations. The process had been going on throughout history and affected every form of life from plants and sea slugs up to the higher animals and even (one must say this in a whisper to oneself) man himself.

It was still going on. In the Argentine pampas, Darwin had witnessed the descendants of the Spanish settlers hunting down the remaining aboriginal Indians, whom they were soon to exterminate completely in this part of South America. The bows and arrows of the Indians were no match for the firearms of the Argentine soldiers, any more than a Galápagos finch with an inferior beak could compete with a bird with one stronger and better adapted to the war for food. Darwin now had a working theory for his task of understanding evolution. He called it natural selection, and he soon began to see that all his various studies over the whole range of organic forms fitted into it. But a tremendous amount of further study was needed before it could be put to the public backed by the overwhelming proof of the countless examples required. He set to work.

At this point we must pause. That natural selection was and is a remarkable explanation of evolution is not to be doubted. What is more questionable is the horror scenario with which Darwin accompanied it, treating this as not merely occasional and often accidental but as essential and inveterate. To him the horror was unavoidable, which was why he averted his gaze from the spectacle of heavily armed soldiers exterminating Indians. It was nature's way. But was it? Here we must look more closely at Darwin's emotional detonator, Malthus's essay. Malthus wrote at the

end of a century in which educated Europeans, especially Englishmen, had become vaguely aware that the population around
them was increasing steadily. Fewer children were dying at birth
or in infancy. Doctors were much more likely to save lives than
hitherto, at every phase of the life cycle. Men and women were
living longer. The evidence of population growth was ubiquitous.
Smallish medieval towns had already expanded into vast cities,
like Liverpool, Glasgow, Birmingham, and Manchester, all of
which were still growing fast. London was inflating itself into a
megalopolis. There were disturbing aspects of this increase,
which was statistically confirmed by censuses, albeit inadequate
ones. The poor were no longer tucked away in the countryside
but were horrifically visible in city streets and burgeoning slums:
long, trailing families of dirty, hungry children, begging and
stealing. Travelers reported similar phenomena elsewhere: in
Naples, for example, the largest city in southern Europe and "the
metropolis of beggars," as one of them put it.

The phenomenon was profoundly disturbing, and the Reverend Thomas Malthus, a Cambridge graduate and wrangler (hon-
ors graduate in math) with a passion for economics, was the first
to articulate this concern. He did so in a dramatic manner that
appealed strongly to the theatrical, emotional side of Darwin's
nature. Malthus's theory had a quite simple statistical basis. Without restraints, the reproductive forces in nature increased in geometrical progression. Food supplies, by contrast, increased only
in arithmetical progression. At the rate we were going, he argued,
the number of mouths would double every twenty-five years.

The amount of food would rise only marginally. The result: mass starvation, famine, pestilence, war, and every kind of catastrophe.

Malthus's aim was to discourage charity and reform the existing poor laws, which, he argued, encouraged the destitute to breed and so aggravated the problem. That was not Darwin's concern. What struck him was the contrast between geometrical progression (breeding) and arithmetical progression (food supplies). Not being a mathematician, he did not check the reasoning and accuracy behind Malthus's law. Was he not a Cambridge wrangler? In fact, Malthus's law was nonsense. He did not prove it. He stated it. What strikes one reading Malthus is the lack of hard evidence throughout. Why did this not strike Darwin? A mystery. Malthus's only "proof" was the population expansion of the United States. In 1750 the total white population was 1 million. In 1775 it was 2 million. In 1800 it was 4.3 million. Here was his evidence of population doubling every twenty-five years, with annual rates reaching 3 percent. But this did not take into account immigration, still less the reason for mass immigration, the opening up of the Midwest, the largest and richest uncultivated arable region in the world, capable of producing grain and livestock for the entire planet. If Malthus had troubled to inquire further, he would have discovered that the food consumption of the United States had been, and was, increasing per capita all the time, in quantity and quality. He might also have discovered that in England and Wales, living standards, especially food consumption, had been increasing throughout the eighteenth century despite the rise in population, thanks largely to the agricultural revolution, which had enormously raised productivity per acre, both in animal and cereal production, as well as bringing more wasteland into use. It was also worth pointing out that in England and Wales, presumably Malthus's chief concern, the population had risen from 5.75 million in 1700 to 6 million in 1750 and then to 9.25 million in 1800. It had not doubled in one hundred years, let alone twenty-five.

Ireland would have been a much better example for Malthus to cite. Its population was rising fast and its dependence on a single crop, the potato, increasing. The Irish population in 1700 had been 2.5 million. By 1750 it was 3 million, and by 1800 it had risen to 4.5 million. So in a century, it had nearly doubled. This was nothing like Malthus's assumption of a doubling every twenty-five years. Had this occurred, the Irish population in 1800 would have been 40 million! In fact the rate of Irish population increase rose after Malthus wrote and undoubtedly was causing concern by 1838 when Darwin read him. In the late 1840s, it produced the kind of catastrophe Malthus predicted. But this was caused by the potato blight, which actually led to more deaths in other countries, such as Poland, where the rise in population was much less. There was no point at which Malthus's geometrical/arithmetical rule could be made to square with the known facts. And he had no reason whatsoever to extrapolate from the high American rates to give a doubling effect every twenty-five years everywhere and in perpetuity.

Quite apart from his tragic ignorance of mathematics, or rather his lack of feeling for figures, it is odd that Darwin should have paid so much attention to this superficial, albeit powerful, tract. Odder still that he should have extrapolated still further than Malthus and applied the geometrical/arithmetical ratio to the whole of organic nature, not just human populations. For in the first place, Darwin knew perfectly well that no clear contrast could be made between organic birth rates and food production, because organic and especially animal matter is always a key element in the food chain, and more births mean more food. Darwin should have known and must (I think) have known that it is often the increase in food that produces the higher birth rates. His grandfather certainly knew this. Furthermore, from his own studies, Darwin was aware how rapidly and spectacularly food supplies could be increased by selective breeding and cultivation. Gooseberries, for instance, about which he knew a lot, had been doubled and quadrupled in size and weight in very much less than twenty-five years. Over the past century, England had produced many striking examples of food supplies in a given acreage rising in geometrical progression. But Darwin did not think about these things. He swallowed Malthusianism because it fitted his emotional need; he did not apply the tests and deploy the skepticism that a scientist should. It was a rare lapse from the discipline of his profession. But it was an important one. Oddly enough, the same mistake was made by his chief competitor in the quest for the answer to the *why* of evolution, Alfred Russel Wallace. He was moving the same way as Darwin by a similar training in different parts of the world, including tropical rain forests, and a little later than Darwin read Malthus, and had a similar shock, which precipitated him toward natural selection. Wallace, too, was no mathematician—quite the contrary. He was also, more so than even Darwin was, emotionally prone to the horror scenario and so fell into the same error. Of course the invalidity of Malthus did not affect the validity of natural selection as a good working theory to show why evolution occurred. But its effect on Darwin, by binding him to that scenario, had malign consequences, to which we shall come.

In the meantime, Darwin, while working hard to extend his investigations into natural selection, planned to raise the population on his own account. He decided to get married. He came to this conclusion at about the same time he read Malthus, in 1838, but whereas his reaction to Malthus was emotional, his pondering on marriage was strictly scientific, or at least cerebral. In July, under the heading "This is the Question," he wrote down the arguments in two parallel columns headed "Marry" and "Not Marry." His not marry considerations were, loss of freedom and "choice of Society," "Loss of Time" and "cannot read in the Evenings" and "less money for books," etc. His "Marry" column was much stronger: "My God it is intolerable to think of spending one's whole life, like a neuter bee, working, working & nothing after all—No, no, won't do." By contrast, "Only picture to yourself a nice soft wife on a sofa with good fire, & books & music perhaps—Compare this Vision with the dingy reality of Grt. Marlbro' St." No doubt about the outcome: "Marry. Q.E.D."

But to whom? This secondary question was not difficult to answer. The enormous Darwin-Wedgwood extended family always had plenty of maids and bachelors available. Darwin soon picked his first cousin Emma, granddaughter of the Wedgwood founder and daughter of the owner of the Maer manor and estate. He proposed on November 11 and was promptly accepted. He called her "the most interesting specimen in the whole series of vertebrate animals." She said, "He is the most open, transparent man I ever saw, and every word expresses his real thoughts." She liked the fact that he was "perfectly sweet tempered," not "fastidious," and "humane to animals." His only fault was that "he has a great dislike to going to the play." Neither had been quick to marry, and both were glad to, Emma being thirty and Charles thirty-one. On both sides, the heads of the family were delighted, and coughed up handsomely. Joshua Wedgwood II pledged £5,000 in investment capital to bring in income plus an annual allowance of £400. The doctor pledged £10,000 to bring in an annual income of £600. Thus the couple began life with the modern equivalent of $1,250,000 in investment capital and an annual income of $83,000. There was every possibility of these sums being substantially increased.

So Charles Darwin's lifelong run of good luck continued. Emma was clever, educated, equable, hardworking, industrious, economical, and not least, sensitive. She provided Darwin with ten children, with considerable effort but without fuss or complaint. She attracted him sexually and continued to do so. This was just as well. His *Beagle* journals show he was highly sexed, noting the Latin American women as "angels gliding down the street," gowns fitting "the figure closely" with "very white silk stockings and very pretty feet," plus "black and brilliant eyes." A new note crept into his scientific jottings as he decided on marriage: "sexual desire makes saliva to flow yes *certainly* . . . one's tendency to kiss, & almost bite, that which one sexually loves is probably connected with flow of saliva, & hence with action of mouth & jaws—Lascivious women are described as biting: so do stallions always." There were also notes on blushing, particularly on the "upper bosom in women," which he compared to "erection" in men.

If Charles and Emma grew to love each other after their marriage rather than before, that was not unusual for the time, and there was no doubt about the reality of the affection when it came. It was a joke between them that marriage was a form of slavery, but a precious kind. Both came from families that for three generations had opposed the slave trade. Emma had always been by upbringing and inclination a passionate antislaver, and Darwin was to become one as a result of what he had witnessed on his travels. So there was a special irony in his references to her as his "chattel," and she, for her part, called him frequently her "nigger" or "hairy nigger." On slavery they were at one, because Darwin carefully avoided raising with her the implications of his division of the races into "civilized" and "savage" ones, and the application of natural selection to the survival or extinction of what he called "inferior" or "lesser" varieties of the human species—"the lower races."

There was, however, no concealing what she called his "materialism" or lack of religious fervor. Like many other educated men of his generation, Darwin had been slowly, almost imperceptibly, but surely, losing religious faith. To what extent this was hastened by his scientific enquiries, it is impossible to say. He did not object to going to church. But he did not read the Bible or believe in it, except the guidance in conduct provided by the New

Testament, whose influence lingered, probably until his death. When he went to Cambridge, he had been reasonably content with the idea of ordination as his future role in life and had been prepared to sign the Anglican Thirty-Nine Articles of Religion. But that was certainly no longer true in the late 1830s. By then his religious posture was best described as indifferent. The word *agnostic*, which best described it, was not coined until 1861 by his follower T. H. Huxley. Emma's use of the term *materialist* was not inaccurate. Darwin was concerned with the physical realities of life on earth and probing their mysteries. He was temperamentally disinclined to probe the possibilities of life after death or to speculate on "salvation." The one point on which he felt strongly, with growing passion as his life proceeded, was the doctrine of everlasting punishment. He thought it not only untrue but positively evil, and he was prepared to say so among his intimates. By contrast, Emma was, had always been, and remained a sincere and trusting Christian, in dogma a curious combination of nonconformist and Anglican—not uncommon at the time, especially among women of her class and cultural background—but in her rules of personal conduct, a believer whose religion was paramount and ubiquitous in guiding her.

Being vaguely aware of all this, the doctor, Darwin's father, advised his son in the summer of 1838, before he proposed to Emma, to conceal his religious doubts from her, now and later. In his experience, a husband who made plain his feelings risked damaging the marriage, especially during those periodic crises, usually caused by ill health, to which all unions were liable. A wife who feared for her husband's salvation through disbelief would worry that the death of either would part them finally for all eternity, and this could become a source of great unhappiness for both. So the doctor advised. But Darwin chose to come clean with Emma and wrote her a letter revealing at least some aspects of his uncertainties. It was this that led her to pronounce him, with strong approval, "transparent." She replied:

> I thank you with all my heart for your openness with me & I should dread the feeling that you were concealing your opinions from me for the fear of giving me pain. It is perhaps foolish of me to say this much but my own dear Charley we now belong to each other & I cannot help being open with you. Will you do me a favour? Yes I am sure you will: it is to read our saviour's farewell discourse to his disciples which begins at the end of the 13th chapter of John. It is so full of love to them & devotion & every beautiful feeling. It is the part of the New Testament I love best. This is a whim of mine—it would give me great pleasure though I can hardly tell you why. I don't wish you to give me your opinion about it.

There the matter rested until, in February 1839 (they were married on January 29), Emma wrote her husband a long letter. It is one of the great love letters of the nineteenth century. It is worth quoting at length both because it radiates wisdom and shows why Emma was such a good wife for Darwin, so important to the success of his mission, and also because the response it evoked in him tells us a lot about Darwin and his nature. She wrote:

The state of mind which I wish to preserve with respect to you, is to feel that while you are acting conscientiously & sincerely wishing, & trying to learn the truth, you cannot be wrong; but there are some reasons that force themselves upon me & prevent my being always able to give myself this comfort. . . . I will write down what has been in my head, knowing that my own dearest will indulge me. Your mind & time are full of the most interesting subjects & thoughts of the most absorbing kind, viz following up yr own discoveries—but which make it very difficult to you to avoid casting out as interruptions other sorts of thoughts which have no relation to what you are pursuing or to be able to give your whole attention to both sides of the question. . . .

May not the habit in scientific pursuits of believing nothing until it is proved, influence your mind too much in other things which cannot be proved in the same way, & which if true are likely to be above our comprehension. I should say also that there is a danger in giving up revelation which does not exist on the other side [of the question], that is, the fear of ingratitude in casting off what has been done for your benefit as well as for that of all the world & which ought to make you more careful, perhaps even fearful lest you should not have taken all the pains you could to judge truly. I do not know if this is arguing as if one side is true & the other false, which I meant to avoid, but I think not. I do not quite agree with you in what you once said—that luckily there were no doubts as to how one ought to act. I think that prayer is an instance to the contrary, in one case it is a positive duty & perhaps not in the other. But I dare say you meant in actions which concern others & then I agree with you almost if not quite. I do not wish for any answer to all this—it is a satisfaction to me to write it & when I talk to you about it I cannot say exactly what I wish to say, & I know you will have patience, with your own dear wife. Don't think it is not my affair and that it does not much signify to me. Every thing that concerns you concerns me & I should be most unhappy if I thought we did not belong to each other forever.

I am rather afraid my own dear Nigger will think I have forgotten my promise not to bother him, but I am sure he loves me & I cannot tell him how happy he makes me & how dearly I love him & thank him for all his affection which makes the happiness of my life more & more every day.

The letter, not notable for its logic—it was, as I say, a love letter— had its effect, in sanctifying the metaphysics of their religious differences and revealing to Darwin the nobility of her nature. He wrote at the end: "When I am dead, know that I have many times kissed and cryed over this—C.D." It is not a letter many wives could have written or many husbands cherished. Among their contemporaries, it is not an exchange that would have been possible between, say, the Gladstones or the Tennysons or the Lincolns. Or between George Eliot and G. H. Lewes, or Jane and Thomas Carlyle, or Professor and Mrs. Huxley, or Charles's brother Erasmus and his then intimate friend Harriet Martineau—just to mention a few couples known to or contemporary with them. The letter and its footnote form an important piece of information about the personal background to Darwin's great work.

Darwin's relationship with his wife, close and tender but characterized by an unbridgeable gap over belief, added an important dimension not to his work as such but to his presentation of it. It complicated and deepened the trauma caused by his profound awareness of the Priestley crisis in his family history and his anxiety not to repeat it. Darwin was not going to allow any religious consideration to impede his scientific work. But he was anxious to avoid, if humanly possible, any open charge of infidelity and, above all, any angry and public conflict. Marriage to Emma enormously increased his anxieties and fears on this point. In fact, the age of Church-and-King riots were over. The coming "No Popery" commotion of the early 1850s, in response to the reinstitution of the Catholic hierarchy in England by the Vatican, though noisy, was a very tame affair compared to the Priestley riot of the early 1790s, let alone the dreadful Gordon Riots of 1780. The Victorian age was altogether more subdued and purely argumentative, even gentlemanly, in expressing its religious differences than the eighteenth century. But Darwin could not bank on this, and his secret terror of becoming involved in a fight with religious fundamentalists was now redoubled by his knowledge of the infinite distress it would cause Emma. It set up a constant anxiety in his mind, and this in turn affected his health.

Apart from seasickness, Darwin had survived his *Beagle*

voyage with his good health intact. The first symptoms of a change occurred on September 20, 1837, when he suffered an "uncomfortable palpitation of the heart," and his doctor, fearing overwork, advised complete rest. During the winter of 1839–40, there was a definite deterioration, and a multitude of symptoms: nausea, vomiting, headaches, stomach pains, rheumatism, heart pain, flatulence, and chronic fatigue. These symptoms and many others persisted at intervals for the rest of his life. His illness, if such a collection of disparate symptoms could be grouped under a single head, was never satisfactorily diagnosed, though Darwin consulted more than a dozen doctors over the years. One sugges- tion was incipient epilepsy. Another was a tropical fever as a result of an insect bite during the *Beagle* years. Darwin's father, who might have solved the mystery, declined to treat him, from a prejudice, common among doctors, against having a member of the family as a patient. He very likely would have concluded the ill- nesses were psychosomatic in origin, provoked by Darwin's worry about his work, the widening breach between natural selection and religion, and the fear of distressing Emma.

One result of Darwin's period of ill health was a move out of London, which Darwin had always felt was a "filthy and noxious place" anyway, with its fogs, smogs, smoke, bad air, and river stench. They found the perfect place in July 1842: Down House, in a small hamlet of the same name near Farnborough in Kent. It was large enough to accommodate a growing family and servants but unpretentious, "built of shabby bricks," with forty acres. It has now been restored, more or less to the condition, inside and out, that it was in when Darwin lived there, and it is open to the public, so those sufficiently interested can see exactly how Darwin spent the last forty years of his life.

Down was intensely quiet and totally secluded then, and Darwin immediately set about increasing the privacy by planting trees. What he wanted, he now decided, was the ability and right to exclude any visitors when he was working intensely or not in the mood to receive them, together with the chance to invite them, for meals, for weekends, or for longer stays, if he felt like it or needed to see savants for professional reasons. The combination of Down, which was only thirteen miles from London, and his "illnesses," which gave him the privileged status of an invalid, exactly met this requirement. The shrewder observers, such as the diarist William Allingham, noted the way in which Darwin used his ill health to produce a mixture of total seclusion and accessibility, another reason for thinking his complaint psychosomatic.

For Darwin, doubtless, it was genuine enough and caused him considerable distress over the years. Indeed, it was the only real misery in an astonishingly fortunate life. It periodically kept him off work, though it should be noted that whenever he particularly wanted and needed to produce material, he always brushed aside sickness. Thus during the ten months when he actually produced the text of *The Origin of Species* as we know it—the only occasion in his life when he was working under compulsion and against the clock—he had an unusual number of sickness fits, five, or one every two months. They were clearly produced by the strain of his work. But he did not allow them to stop his writing.

Darwin made various ingenious and frustrated efforts to cure himself, using new "scientific" techniques that appealed to his intellect. For one, the water cure, he submitted himself to a Dr. Gully, of the Spa at Malvern, for a sixteen-week program. For this he rented a house, The Lodge, Malvern (still to be seen). He was denied sugar, salt, bacon, and alcohol and had wet compresses placed on his stomach all day, changed every two hours. This did not cure him permanently, but he felt it did him good. And he liked it. So back at Down, he built himself a douche hut near the three-hundred-foot-deep well in the garden. This had a cistern that held 640 gallons of water. With the help of his butler, Parslow, or his *Beagle* valet Syms Covington (until the latter went to Australia), he had a huge shower, through a two-inch pipe, every day, and a plunge bath every hour. Between plunges he took exercise along a 250-yard track known as the Sandwalk, which he laid down in the garden. This water cure, undertaken in many different forms, was further varied by a novel system known as the ice cure, in which bags of ice, frequently changed, were pressed against his back for periods of ninety minutes each. In one way or another, these modish techniques, which included electric shocks, were enjoyed by Darwin for forty years. He seems to have liked them partly at least because they involved a regular and satisfying routine.

Darwin loved routine. At Down House, he had regular timetables, which of course changed a little in accordance with his work or medical treatment, but almost imperceptibly. One went as follows. A walk on rising at between 6:30 A.M. and 7:00 A.M. Breakfast at 7:30 A.M. Work at 8:00 A.M. for ninety minutes. Then an hour's writing of letters (he wrote probably over twenty thousand, a large proportion of which have survived and have been published). At 10:30 A.M., there was a further ninety-minute work period. Then at noon, a medicinal shower, followed by the Sandwalk and a visit to the greenhouses, which were extensive and involved scientific plantings vital to his work. Then came luncheon (as he called it), a glance through the newspapers (the *Times, Morning Post,* and *Daily News*), a further session of letter-writing, a rest, during which a novel was often read to him, and a thirty-minute walk. At 4:30 P.M., a sixty-minute work period began, followed by a social half hour in the drawing room talking to the family and visitors. Then came another ninety-minute rest period, high tea at 7:30 P.M. (this was partly a result of Darwin's Midland upbringing, where the main meal was usually taken at lunch, confusingly called *dinner*). After that came backgammon, usually with Emma, reading scientific books and periodicals, and bed at 10:30 P.M. Characteristically, Darwin kept a careful record of his gambling (only for points, not money). He told an American correspondent in 1876 that, so far, he had won 2,795 games of backgammon; Emma, 2,490.

Gradually Darwin made Down a house and workplace of exactly the kind he wished. His income was periodically increased by his generous father and, despite a growing family, there were years in which a good half of it was saved and reinvested. It is curious to us that Darwin did not employ a clever young man as an assistant, preferably one with modern language skills who could have combed through the current scientific publications, especially those in German. He could well have afforded such help, and his failure to do so was to prove costly. He spent money, however, on making his kitchen garden, hothouses, and woods an adjunct of his study in housing all the plants and creatures he wished to observe and record.

The arrival of children at regular intervals delighted him. Unlike many studious men, especially scientists, Darwin never regarded children, especially his own, as a nuisance or a distraction. On the contrary, he tried to give them employment. When working on bees, he placed each child (he then had six available) at special points along routes he thought bees took in their search for suitable flowers. He dusted each plant with flour, which adhered to the bee's body, and told the children to shout out each time a bee with flour on it reached another plant. This was one of dozens of experiments in which we know he involved them. His son Leonard, when three, was observed going out in the garden to look at a flower and, when questioned, replied, "I've a fact to do."

Darwin was especially kind to children when they were ill. Any sick child had the right to lie covered in blankets on the sofa in his study. The deaths of three of his ten children were painful tragedies to him. The one that hit him the hardest was the fatal sickness of his favorite child, Annie, which began in June 1850, when she was nine, and ended in her death the following April when she was ten. We have a good photograph of her taken two years before her death. She obviously very much resembled her mother, but Darwin loved her primarily because of her goodness and the sweetness of her nature—"a perfect angel." The inexorable progress of her mysterious malady is recorded in detail in letters and notebooks. Darwin felt a huge burden of guilt because he believed her trouble was inherited from himself. She was subjected to the water cure under Dr. Gully, wet-sheet wrappings every two hours, rubbing of the back with a saturated towel, showers and pumpings, and ice-cold baths, especially of her feet and hands. Then, not responding, she was taken to Malvern, but nothing availed. On April 23, 1851, Darwin wrote to Emma, at Down:

> She went to her final sleep most tranquilly, most sweetly at 12 o'clock today. Our poor dear dear child has had a very short life but I trust happy, & God only knows what miseries might have been in store for her. She expired without a sigh. How desolate it makes one to think of her frank cordial manners ... I cannot remember ever seeing the dear child naughty. God bless her ... my own poor dear dear wife.

Emma's diary simply recorded: "12 o'clock." It is notable that Darwin's letters during the final phase were one long prayer to God for her recovery. He mentions God fourteen times in his letter to Emma; she, only twice. The blow was the worst single torment in his entire life, exceeding in pain even the death of his mother. He was too distraught to attend the little girl's funeral. He never forgot her, and he never forgave God for taking her away. The cruelty, as he saw it, blew away the last vestige of his belief in a benign deity. What Leibniz had called theodicy, the notion of divine justice, no longer made any sense to him, and thereafter, though without admitting it to Emma, he carried on his work as though God did not exist. The final collapse of his belief, be it noted, had nothing to do with scientific discovery: It was purely a matter of intimate loss. But he now possessed no personal religious reason, on his own account—leaving aside his respect for Emma's feelings—for avoiding the direst conclusion to his work on evolution by nature alone. From 1851 his work took on an extra intensity and vehemence.

CHAPTER FOUR

The Making of a Masterpiece

Nearly a quarter of a century elapsed between Darwin's return from the *Beagle* voyage and the publication of *The Origin of Species* in 1859. It may be asked: What exactly was he doing during these years, the best in his life in terms of intellectual maturity and physical energy? He opened his notebooks on transmutations in 1837. He hit upon his working theory of natural selection in 1838. He saw himself as collecting material for his great book so as to present his theory backed by overwhelming evidence, and it is certainly true that he amassed an ever growing pile of facts about the way organisms grew. As he put it, "I am like Croesus, overwhelmed by my riches of facts." The term *overwhelmed* was apt. Like many other scholars of all times, Darwin accumulated more material than he could ever possibly have needed. He never acquired the basic economic theory of research: an overprovision of material and evidence is not only unnecessary but a positive hindrance to a completed work.

In fact, he began to sketch his theory of natural selection as the means by which species were varied and created as early as 1842 and completed it in 1844. Why did he not publish it sooner, in some form? Why wait fifteen years? There were two reasons, both tinged by fear. If there was one possible judgment that terrified Darwin, it was that his conclusions about natural selection would be dismissed as "mere speculation." In mid-Victorian times, it was the deadliest phrase to be used about innovative science and was frequently employed. Hence he was determined to accumulate the maximum possible number of examples that fitted his working theory before making it public. The second reason was less admirable. Darwin's fear of the Priestley factor, compounded by the don't-upset-Emma factor, compelled him, almost despite himself, to go on accumulating examples as a way of delaying the need to publish. This, too, is not an uncommon phenomenon in research.

Besides, it is a fact made overwhelmingly clear by Darwin's research notebooks that he took great delight in investigating, dissecting, classifying, and recording organic things and creatures. And the smaller they were, the more he liked it. It is a curious reflection on the emphasis of his research that he never did any serious research on vertebrates. He made no real attempt to become an expert anthropologist. He was interested in facial expressions and observed his children carefully as they became old enough to exhibit them. He studied, for comparison, the emotions of any available animal, such as his dog Bob, noting his "Hot House Face," for example. But that, plus occasional visits to the zoo, was as far as it went. The arrival of the first gorilla in England, paraded in Wombwell's Circus, which was a sensation in 1855, aroused surprisingly little interest in him. The emergence of evidence about Neanderthal man, soon after, also did not fascinate him as one might have expected.

On the other hand, he spent many years working on small or minute creatures or on other species that caught his fancy—orchids, for instance, for which he built a special heated greenhouse, and pigeons and spiders. He loved minute things. He wrote: "The brain of an ant is one of the most marvellous atoms of matter in the world." He was prodigal of the time he devoted to watching ants at work. He particularly admired their system of slavery: why they adopted it, the types of slaves they sought and how they were managed, the way in which ant slaves became so accustomed to the system that they helped the master ants to uphold it, and many other aspects. It was one of his many contradictions that he took objective delight in slavery practiced by ants, as an illustration of natural selection at work, while bitterly deploring it among humans. He spent eight years working on barnacles, longer than on any other subject in his whole life. He had first found them interesting on the *Beagle*. His close friend Dr. Hooker told Darwin's son Francis, who eventually wrote his life, "Your father had barnacles on the brain from Chile onwards." He referred to them as "my beloved barnacles." He sent for specimens from all over the world and bought a special compound microscope to help in dissecting them. For the first and perhaps only time, he became expert in the work of dissection. The movements of his hands became quick and neat and were a pleasure to watch. In a letter to his old chief, FitzRoy, he said he had been "for the last half-month daily hard at work in dissecting a little animal about the size of a pin's-head, from the Chonos archipelago, and I could spend another month, and daily see more beautiful structure." This barnacle study was the most thorough piece of scientific investigation Darwin ever carried through to completion—in four stout volumes published over the years 1851–54—and he convinced himself it was vital to his evolutionary work. The letter to Hooker in which he justified this is worth quoting:

> I have lately got a bisexual cirripede [barnacle], the male being microscopically small & parasitic within the sac of the female. I tell you this to boast of my species theory, for the nearest & closely allied genus to it is, as usual, hermaphrodite, but I had observed some minute parasites adhering to it, & these parasites, I now can show, are supplemental males, the male organs in the hermaphrodite being unusually small, though perfect and containing zoosperms: so we have almost a polygamous animal, simple females alone being wanting. I never should have made this out, had not my species theory convinced me, that an hermaphrodite species must pass into a bisexual species by insensible small stages, and here we have it.

The work on barnacles brought him the medal of the Royal Society in 1853, but the eight years spent on it made no sense in terms of the work structure of *Origin*. Again, there were his "beloved orchids." He wrote defensively to Hooker: "I have found the study of orchids eminently useful in showing me how nearly all parts of the flower are coadapted for fertilization by insects, & therefore the results of natural selection." This work on orchids was relevant to *Origin*, though the manuscript, under the title *On the Various Contrivances by Which British and Foreign Orchids are Fertilised by Insects*, was not actually published till three years after the masterwork to which its details (filling 140 large folio pages in

Darwin's small handwriting) were supposedly preliminary. It was the same with pigeons. He wrote to one of his sons: "I am getting on splendidly with my pigeons and the other day had a present of Trumpeters, Nuns and Turbits, and when last in London I visited a jolly old brewer, who keeps 300 or 400 most beautiful pigeons and he gave me a pair of pale brown, quite small German Pouters. I am building a new House for my Tumblers, so as to fly them in summer." These birds gave him delight, but their contribution to *Origin* clearly did not justify the time he spent on them. The truth is, he pursued these lines of research for their own sake but also because they inevitably delayed the day when he would have to "go public" with his general theory of evolution and natural selection and thus detonate the crisis of his personal, professional, religious, and, indeed, marital life.

Meanwhile, as Darwin delayed by over-research and the years went by, other scientists and writers were pressing on and publishing, and evolution itself was becoming almost a hackneyed subject. The most important event came in 1844, when an anonymous work appeared called *Vestiges of the Natural History of Creation*. It caused an uproar, was a bestseller, and was in its twelfth edition by 1884 when its author, long dead, was at last officially identified. He was the Edinburgh publisher Robert Chambers, a polymath seven years Darwin's senior, who had spent two years collecting scientific facts to show (among other things) that the Genesis account of creation could not be taken literally. Chambers went to elaborate lengths to maintain secrecy, not wishing to get involved in religious quarrels (he remained a stalwart Christian till his death in 1871) or damage his business. The effect of his book was to make evolution appear almost "normal" among the educated and to act as a lightning rod to deflect any real chance of combustion by the time *Origin* was published fifteen years later (by then over two hundred thousand copies of *Vestiges* were circulating). Darwin himself wrote of it: "In my opinion it has done excellent service in this country in calling attention to the subject, in removing prejudice, and in thus preparing the ground for the reception of analogous views." By the mid-1840s, the idea that species "evolved" or "developed," as opposed to being created in an instant by God, was so common that Disraeli, always smart and quick to pounce on a fashionable fad, was happy to satirize it in his novel *Tancred* (1847) and have his heroine say, "You know, all is development. The principle is perpetually going on. First there was nothing. Then there was something. Then—I forget the next—I think there were shells, then fishes. Then we came—let me see—did we come next? Never mind that—we came at last." This, one suspects, is more or less how a good many society ladies felt about the matter. Disraeli returned to the subject, again in ironic mood, in *Lothair* (1870).

However, it was Darwin's exact contemporary, Tennyson, who glorified and almost sanctified evolution in his great poem *In Memoriam* (1851), the work that established him as a major poet, indeed *the* major poet and the natural successor to Wordsworth as poet laureate. Although Tennyson is often superficially regarded as the poet of Arthurian legend, he had the mind of a naturalist and observed natural phenomena not only with admiration but with accurate objectivity: It was he who coined the Darwinian phrase "nature red in tooth and claw." It might be said that the study of nature was an obsession for literate and clever early

Victorians, such as John Ruskin and George Eliot. She, like Darwin, was particularly obsessed by the foreshore and its creatures and spent a holiday at Ilfracombe in Devon investigating barnacles and seaweed. She read Lyell, as well as the *Vestiges,* and was an evolutionist by the time she was nineteen. She greatly admired the brilliant young polymath Herbert Spencer, another evolutionist (both were a decade younger than Darwin), and actually went so far as to write him a letter proposing marriage, which filled him with terror and put him off matrimony for good. Dickens was another such; he wrote an admiring review in the *Examiner* of the anonymous *The Poetry of Science; or, Studies in the Physical Phenomena of Nature,* which was actually by Dr. Robert Hunt of the School of Mines. Dickens's journalism was spattered with admiring references to *Vestiges.* Such people came to look up to Tennyson as their poetic oracle, and *In Memoriam* was exactly in the spirit of the times (next to the decade 1810–20, the 1850s was the most creative period in nineteenth-century England) in its most ardent curiosity and sensitivity to nature, accepting evolution but also soothing doubts. Tennyson wrote:

> I held it truth, with him who sings
>> To one clear harp in divers tones.
>> That men may rise on stepping stones
>> Of their dead selves to higher things.

He also conjured up the eternal permanence of love between man and man, as with Arthur Hallam (tragic hero of the poem) and the whole process of evolution:

So then were nothing lost to man;
　　So that still garden of the souls
　　In many a figured leaf enrolls
The total world since life began.

He said that "good / Will be the final goal of ill;"

　　That nothing walks with aimless feet;
　　　　That not one life shall be destroy'd,
　　　　Or cast as rubbish to the void,
　　When God hath made the pile complete;

　　That not a worm is cloven in vain;
　　　　That not a moth with vain desire
　　　　Is shrivell'd in a fruitless fire,
　　Or but subserves another's gain.

Tennyson admitted the seeming cruelty of nature—"So careful of
the type she seems / So careless of the single life"—and that it
was easy to see all creation as an exercise in nihilism, for nature
cries, "A thousand types are gone; / I care for nothing, all shall
go." Still, the message of the poem, which might be construed as
a hymn to evolution, is that the ultimate phase of evolution will be
beneficent. G. M. Young rightly called *In Memoriam* a "cardinal
document of the mid-Victorian mind, with Tennyson 'speaking
like an Archangel' assuring mankind that it will muddle through."

Among those who loved *In Memoriam* and saw the point of its
view of evolution was Queen Victoria, for whom Tennyson was

the greatest living poet. It was one reason evolution never presented a problem to her. Prince Albert, too, was an evolutionist. In fact rumor had it that he was the author of *Vestiges*.

An outspoken and vigorous exponent of evolution was the young Herbert Spencer, a former railway engineer and self-made polymath, whose key article in the *Leader*, on "The Development Hypothesis" (1852) came soon after the appearance of Tennyson's poem. He took the clerical critics head on. They accused evolutionists of lacking evidence from facts, he wrote, while seeming to forget

that their own theory [Genesis] is supported by no facts at all. Like the majority of men who are born to a given belief, they demand the most rigorous proof of any adverse doctrine, but assume that their own doctrine needs none. . . . From the earliest appearance of life down to the present time, different species have been successively replacing each other [and] we may safely estimate the number of species that have existed, or are existing, on the earth, at not less than ten million. Well, which is the most rational theory? . . . Is it most likely that there have been ten million of special creations? Or is it most likely that, by continual modifications, due to change of circumstances, ten millions of varieties may have been produced, as varieties are being produced still?

Spencer is largely forgotten now and certainly little read. But at the time, he was regarded as the great and coming panjandrum.

Darwin thought he would eventually be looked on "as by far the greatest living philosopher in England; perhaps equal to any that have lived." In his *Principles of Biology*, he coined the phrase "survival of the fittest," which Darwin eventually adopted in his fifth edition of the *Origin*.

Spencer was a great gobbler-up, appropriator, and popularizer of others' ideas. By the mid-1850s, he was the best-known exponent of evolution and might easily have gobbled up natural selection, if he had been aware of it. Lyell, whom Darwin treated as his closest confidant and who was kept fully aware of his growing conviction that natural selection was the *why* of evolution, became perturbed at Darwin's continual delay in publishing his thesis. He wrote to him, warning him strongly that there was a danger he would be "forestalled" and lose all the credit for his work and originality. And it is a fact that others had been moving in precisely this train of thought. As far back as January 1831, before Darwin set out on the *Beagle*, Patrick Matthew had published a book, *Naval Timber and Arboriculture*, which set out the theory of the selection of the fittest by nature, in the reproductive process, quite clearly, in a ten-line paragraph. This was widely reviewed, though Darwin had never nor had, as he claimed, "any other naturalist," ever heard of Matthew's views. This was not quite true. John Claudius Loudon, the famous horticulturalist, had reviewed the book in the *Gardeners' Chronicle*. Nor was Matthew, as Darwin claimed, an obscure writer on forest trees. He was a large-scale commercial grower of fruit trees in Scotland, who ran a ten-thousand-tree orchard and knew all about the highly relevant subject of hybridizing. Fortunately for Darwin, he was a modest man who was ready to claim his priority when *Origin* came out but did not make a fuss. He wrote that natural selection "to me did not appear a discovery . . . I estimated this select production of species as an a priori recognizable fact—an axiom, requiring only to be pointed out to be admitted by unprejudiced minds of sufficient grasp."

There was also the case of Edward Blyth, a naturalist with long experience in India, who was not only known to Darwin but regularly corresponded with him. Blyth wrote a number of articles in the 1830s in the *Magazine of Natural History*, arguing that the work of breeders was also performed by nature in selecting the best, and suggesting that "a large proportion of what are considered species have descended from a common parentage." In a number of ways, Blyth's writings covered the same ground as Darwin's, who copied Blyth's arguments in his preliminary treatments of 1842–44. The fact that Blyth believed that natural selection would also tend to conserve species was presumably Darwin's reason (or excuse) for not giving him any credit in his introduction to the third edition of *Origin*, in which he mentions earlier workers in the field. Darwin was an honest and generous man in general—there is no doubt about that—but his behavior toward Matthew and Blyth does raise questions about his sense of justice.

In 1856 Lyell again urged Darwin to publish. He had read a paper published the previous September in the *Annals and Magazine of Natural History* entitled "On the Law which has Regulated the Introduction of New Species." The author was Alfred Russel Wallace, who had become interested in evolution when reading *Vestiges* and had spent years collecting information in the Amazon and the Malay Archipelago. Other experts, Darwin's old friend Hooker and two new ones, Thomas Henry Huxley and Thomas Vernon Wollaston, also urged publication. Darwin worked on doggedly—"It's dogged as does it" was one of his favorite sayings—and the book he planned to be published eventually, but possibly not for many years, was to have been enormous.

However, on June 18, 1859, or possibly on May 18—the point is subject to much debate—he received a letter and manuscript from Wallace that alarmed him. Like Darwin, Wallace had read Malthus, in about 1836. Early in 1858, he had a bout of malaria, and during his delirium, he remembered Malthus's horror scenario and saw how it fitted into the evolution problem. He called it "a sudden flash of insight." When he recovered, he set down his view of natural selection in a four-thousand-word paper and sent it to Darwin, rather than to a learned journal, asking him to use it as he judged proper. Darwin was deeply shocked and sent it to Lyell: "Your words have come true with a vengeance—that I should be forestalled." He said that the Wallace paper might have been a digest of his 1842 sketch or serve as the chapter heads for his current huge tome, so close was the correspondence of the ideas. Lyell was told, "So all my originality, whatever it may amount to, will be smashed." His only consolation was that his huge efforts would not be wasted, "as all the labour consists in the application of the theory." He added, "I would far rather burn my whole book than that Wallace or any other man should think that I have behaved in a paltry spirit."

Lyell consulted Hooker, and they agreed that the fairest solution was to use a forthcoming meeting of the Linnean Society on

July 1 to make public the theory of natural selection by reading out, and later printing in the society's journal, contributions by both Wallace and Darwin. Three documents were read: Wallace's essay, Darwin's 1844 paper, and an 1857 letter outlining his theory to his friend and confidant at Harvard, Professor Asa Gray. Darwin's friends were eager to publicize the fact that he had priority in the idea, so his main contribution was described as "Extract from a MS. work on Species, by Charles Darwin Esq., FRS, FLS, &c., sketched in 1839 and copied in 1844." Darwin could not be present, as his son Charles had just died from scarlet fever, and other members of his family were ill.

As it happened, neither the meeting nor subsequent publication attracted much attention, even in the professional world, let alone among the general public. The multiplicity of the papers was a handicap to understanding, and it was all too complex and technical for listeners to take in. In fact, Wallace's intervention was an astounding stroke of luck for Darwin, typical of the good fortune that attended him throughout his life. For it did stir him into action of precisely the kind required. He began to write, with all deliberate speed, a general account of evolution by natural selection, that could be understood by the public and contained in one reasonable-sized volume. Instead of an enormous, multivolume work published over a number of years and containing much technical detail as well as a daunting academic apparatus of footnotes, sources, and bibliography, Darwin found himself hustled into producing a popular treatment. In what we have seen to be a remarkably lucky life, this was the greatest stroke of good fortune he enjoyed.

The first edition of *Origin* was published on November 24, 1859, under the title *On the Origin of Species by Means of Natural Selection; or, The Preservation of Favoured Races in the Struggle for Life*. It was 155,000 words, roughly the same length as *Emma*, Jane Austen's longest novel, or *Great Expectations*, one of Dickens's shorter ones. Its size was similar to two other highly successful treatments of difficult subjects, J. M. Keynes's *The General Theory of Employment, Interest and Money*, and A. J. Ayers's *Language, Truth and Logic*. In proposing it to John Murray, who had published the popular edition of the *Beagle* voyage, Darwin wrote:

> The *book* ought to be popular with a large body of scientific and semi-scientific readers, as it bears on agriculture, the history of our domestic productions and on the whole fields of Zoology, Botany and Geology. . . . I have been quite surprised at finding how much interested strangers and acquaintances have been in the subject. Only some small portions are at all abstruse.

This was a very shrewd estimate. Indeed, once Darwin had decided to take the plunge and publish a popular version of his theory, all his actions—writing, publishing, promoting, and marketing—were highly professional and wholeheartedly directed to making *Origin* the greatest success, both with the scientific elite and the public. The text, in particular, was a nicely judged blend, which mingled clarity and comprehensibility with professional vernacular and decorum, calculated not to offend experts by writing down, or laymen by jargon. The only concession was a useful glossary of terms. Otherwise the entire book was without academic mystification or scaffolding.

There was a brief introduction, in which Darwin cleverly apologized for not quoting his sources or acknowledging his precursors (after the book became a success, he added a "Historical Introduction" for later editions). Then followed fourteen chapters, each headed by a digest of contents and usually ending with a short summary. The first chapter was on domestication, showing how human breeding had produced variations of species in plants and animals. The second describes how variations occur under nature. The third is entitled "Struggle for Existence" and describes the background against which species develop the means of survival. Chapter 4, "Natural Selection," is the argumentative core of the book, concluding with the "grouping of all organic beings" into one endless chain of descent. There follow chapters on "Laws of Variation," answers to "Difficulties on Theory," on instinct as a force in evolution, on hybridism, on the geological record and its "imperfection," on the geological succession of organic beings, on their geographical distribution (two chapters), and on classification. The final chapter is entitled "Recapitulation and Conclusion." Darwin was evidently conscious throughout of the less tutored reader and was eager to help him (or her, as the book had an unusually high percentage of women readers); he was also mindful of the clerical or religious objector, answering difficulties as he went along. No scientific innovator has ever taken more trouble to smooth the way for lay readers without descending into vulgarity. What is almost miraculous about the book is Darwin's generosity in sharing his thought processes, his lack of condescension. There is no talking down, but no hauteur, either. It is a gentlemanly book.

There are four particular reasons for its success with the reader. First, from start to finish, it is a long, sustained argument. This is a very difficult thing to accomplish in a book of 155,000 words, and it would have been quite impossible if Darwin had published at the much greater length he originally intended. The reader is made to feel he is taking part in a great adventure of the mind and gets a thrill of accomplishment in following it step-by-step.

Second, Darwin makes it unconsciously easier by the large number of examples he gives from botany and zoology. People love plants and animals and delight in their peculiarities and exoticisms. Darwin gives plenty of both from the vast range of his knowledge. Neither Wallace nor any other naturalist then active could have managed so wide and fluent a process of vivid illustration. He is, of course, generous with topics he knows will fascinate, especially, for instance, bees running their hives and ants managing their slaves.

Third, Darwin deals with the problem of God and revelation with fine judgment and exquisite tact. He does not offend the strict scientists by ducking the issue. He repeatedly points to the higher probability of selection by nature over creation. He is never actually cowardly. On the other hand, he is never provocative. He avoids the issue of man's descent almost entirely. Only in the third paragraph from the end of the book does he predict that "in the distant future," psychology and mental power will be investigated, and "light will be thrown on the origin of man and his history." We have to distinguish between what Darwin actually wrote and what people read into the book. It is clear, from the first week *Origin* was published, that everyone concluded man was inevitably part of the theory. It was their first reaction on finishing the book. But Darwin nowhere says that man was descended from apes. What he does say, in his last two paragraphs, is designed to be reassuring and uplifting. We can all "look with some confidence to a secure future." Natural selection, he insists, "works solely by and for the good of each being" and "all mental endowments will tend to progress towards perfection." That was exactly what the Victorian public, with its love of reform and improvement, wished to hear. And better followed. Nature might be in perpetual war, said Darwin, but from this struggle the evolution of "higher animals" directly followed. So "there is grandeur in this view of life, with its several powers, having been originally breathed into a few forms or into one."

The final sentence concludes that, while the planet has gone "cycling on according to the fixed law of gravity, from so simple a beginning endless forms most beautiful and most wonderful have been, and are being evolved." This highly optimistic ending thus managed to encompass both the reassuring certitude of Newtonian cosmology and, with the phrase "breathed into," an echo of Genesis and what most readers would have seen as a reference to God as prime mover.

Origin, then, was a cleverly written, superbly presented, and even a cunningly judged book, and quite apart from its veracity deserved to have an enormous impact and sell widely. But it was, and is, open to one objection. This springs from the original excitement and emotion in which Darwin conceived his theory of natural selection, the combination of the impact upon him of the Tierra del Fuegan "savages," the Galápagos beaks, the coral atolls, and Malthus's tract. His emotions convinced him that the "horror scenario" was the way nature operated, and he imparted this feeling to his book. The result, in the long term, was to have malign, even catastrophic, consequences. It is not that Darwin was able to demonstrate that all improvements in a species, or most, or even some of them, are the result of continual warfare and destruction. He gives very few examples of the horrific destructiveness of nature and certainly never demonstrates, by an overwhelming evidence of examples, that nature invariably or habitually or even often exacts a terrible price in suffering for each forward step. He does not do so because he never possessed such evidence. It was always an assumption. What he does do, and it is highly effective in conveying an impression of endless antagonism within and between species, is to use a selective, repetitive and emotional vocabulary of strife.

Occasionally Darwin gives a dramatic picture of natural warfare, as in his description of the primeval American forest in the chapter "Struggle for Existence":

What a struggle between the several kinds of trees must have gone on over long centuries . . . what war between insect and insect—between insects, snails and other animals, with birds and beasts of prey—all striving to increase, and all feeding on each other or on the trees or their seeds and seedlings, or on the other plants which first clothed the grounds and thus checked the growth of the trees!

As a rule, however, the effect is achieved by pitting the text with key words and phrases, all bellicose or militaristic. The word *struggle* is found on almost every page, sometimes two or three times. The "struggle for existence," the "race for life," the "battle for life," and "great battle for life" crop up continually. We hear again and again of "forces," "war between insect and insect," "invasion," "intruders," of "foreigners" who are "taking possession of the land," of plants and animals being "rigidly destroyed," of constant "attacks," of species being "beaten" or being "victorious." The words *destroy, extinct,* and *extermination* occur many times. Malthus rears his misleading head repeatedly: his "doctrine" of births proceeding "in geometrical ratio"—a term Darwin uses repeatedly without ever explaining what he means by it or how he justifies employing it. All he says is that "it applies with manifest truth to the whole animal and vegetable kingdom." He terrifies the reader with a vision of "fifteen million elephants" suddenly appearing if these creatures—whom he picks as the slowest in procreating—are allowed to do so unchecked, and he has further catastrophic visions of the earth so crowded with animals that none could move. Hence the need for continual and colossal killings.

As it happens, Darwin, displaying the ambiguity that was one of his most marked characteristics, quails before the bloodthirsty visions he conjures up and tries to comfort the terrified reader by softening them in such a way as to refute much of what he has just said. Thus at one point, he suddenly states that climate, rather than war within or between species, is by far the greatest check on numbers, thus shoving the battle scenario offstage. At another, he abruptly announces that "natural selection will always act very slowly, often only at long intervals of time, and generally on only a very few of the inhabitants of the same region at the same time." This is a very different picture from the incessant struggle that he portrays elsewhere, which forms the general impression left with the reader. The truth, of course, is that the fossil record gives no evidence of struggle, and Darwin's next sentence shows why he introduced the qualification: "This very slow, intermittent action of natural selection accords perfectly well with what geology tells us of the rate and manner at which the inhabitants of this world have changed."

These qualifications produced a visual image of natural selection that accorded much more closely with the detailed evidence of its operation among both vegetable and animal life. But it was a much less exciting one. The picture that prevailed in readers' minds was the horror/war version, and this was the final factor in making *Origin* the huge success it became, and remains. To this we now turn.

CHAPTER FIVE

Among the Apes and Angels

The *Origin of Species* was sold to the trade on November 22, 1859, and immediately fully subscribed at 1,250 copies, and a new imprint of 3,000 was ordered for January. It was available to the public from November 25. The timing could not have been better. Everyone was talking about race, for the United States was moving toward civil war on the issue of slavery and whether the Southern states had the right to maintain it. A week after the book came out, John Brown was hanged, and his body was marching on in the minds of men and women on both sides of the Atlantic, even before the famous song was composed. Two notable books published earlier in the year had prepared the way. John Stuart Mills's *Essay on Liberty*, the classic statement on the right to hold and publish dissenting opinions, gave powerful intellectual support to Darwin's scientific challenge to religious orthodoxy. And Samuel Smiles's *Self-Help*, a bestseller that soon was to winch up a record sale of 220,000 copies, was a salutary tale of how able, industrious, and dedicated people rose to wealth and fame: how the fittest not only survived but prospered.

It is astonishing how quickly the intellectual elite possessed themselves of *Origin*. George Eliot's diary of November 23 records that she and her partner, George Lewes "began reading Darwin's work Origin of Species tonight." She was critical: "It seems not to be well-written: though full of interesting matter, it is not impressive, from want of luminous and orderly presentation." Later she became more favorable and eventually enthusiastic, though she was worried by what she called its determinism. Lewes wrote a long and widely circulated article welcoming the book—a piece that delighted Darwin. Marx and Engels were both reading it the week of publication and exchanging views. Marx was enthusiastic, as the book was "a basis in natural science for the class struggle in history," and he determined to use the theory of natural selection as a weapon in his ideological war. In a letter on January 28, 1860, Jane Carlyle reported that "Darwin, in a Book that all the scientific world is in ecstasy over, *proved* the other day, that we all come from shell-fish!" But "I did not feel that the slightest light would be thrown on my practical life for me by having it ever so logically made out, that my first ancestor millions of millions of ages back had been, or even had *not* been, an oyster!" She complained bitterly of being pushed into reading a similar book by a woman, Isabelle Duncan's *Pre-Adamite Man*. Letters and diaries of November–January 1859–60, of which dozens mention the *Origin*, make it clear that despite Darwin's deliberate avoidance of the issue of man's descent, everyone took up the ape-into-man issue, and the cartoonists soon followed, delighted by their discovery that Darwin, with his beetling brows, could easily be caricatured as an ape.

Darwin, it turned out, was a superb self-publicist, all the more effective because others did the promotion for him, and he could never be detected in pushing his own work. But over the years, he had developed a huge network of scientific friends and correspondents, and now many of them rallied to him. The text of *Origin* discreetly and ingeniously encouraged this camaraderie. Though Darwin did not use footnotes, he refers to dozens of other active scientists in the text, often with a generous word of praise. One has published "a grand work," another has "forcibly" or "brilliantly" or "luminously" explained a problem. The tone is not exactly sycophantic, but it comes close. And these savants reciprocated. In America, Professor Asa Gray, Darwin's chief supporter there, held a meeting at Harvard as early as May 1859 to announce to scholars in the field that Darwin's book would shortly be published and to give a résumé of its contents. Lyell conducted a similar prepublication exercise at the summer 1859 annual meeting of the British Association for the Advancement of Science. This was one reason sales of the book got off to such a good start. Reviews were mixed, of course, but the expected onslaught did not take place. And there were some remarkable accolades, chiefly delivered by members of Darwin's network. Thomas Henry Huxley, who did not agree with everything in *Origin* by any means at this point, was determined to be pugnaciously on Darwin's side as a matter of simple team spirit, scientists versus clerics.

By a stroke of luck, the regular *Times* reviewer was unwilling to get involved and gladly handed over his task to Huxley, who used the opportunity for all it was worth. This was a period when the *Times*, under the great John Delane, was the most influential publication in the country. Moreover, as the *Times* review was anonymous, Huxley was able to do a further enthusiastic review, under his own name, in the *Westminster.* Asa Gray provided one of the longest and most helpful reviews in the *Atlantic Monthly,*

America's most important periodical. This was spread over three monthly issues, each installment containing four thousand words. Naturally Darwin was pleased, and his stealthy self-promoting instincts were thoroughly roused. He got the entire twelve-thousand-word accolade reprinted in London as a pamphlet, five hundred copies of which were run off and distributed by him to every reputable library, laboratory, and scientific institution in the country and to large numbers of individual scholars and opinion formers. He compiled lists of learned men in two columns, one "for," the other "against," and noted with satisfaction that the list of savants on his side was longer, and lengthening. Darwin was quite clear that if he could get significant scientists of repute to acknowledge the value of his work (they did not need to agree with all or even most of his conclusions), then it would survive and prosper. He was quite convinced from the start that the younger men would appreciate, and most would follow, him. It was the older men he feared.

Chief among them was Richard Owen, the leading anatomist in Britain. All Darwin's considerable efforts to befriend, placate, and conciliate Owen, and the compliments he paid him, all the favorable mentions in *Origin*, were to no avail. He has been called "an implacable enemy" of Darwin's. This is not true. He gave the book a critical analysis in the *Edinburgh Review*, but it was reasoned, not exactly hostile, and certainly not malicious. The worst he ever said of Darwin was (to Charles Kingsley): "Darwin is just as good a soul as his grandfather—and just as great a goose." But Darwin eventually came to hate Owen, the only scientist toward whom he felt bitter, and regretted his previous civility and hospitality: "I am getting more savage against him," he wrote. "He ought to be ostracized by every Naturalist in England."

What is clear, in general, is that *Origin* met much less hostility than Darwin had always feared. There was no abuse at all. Still less was there any organized attempt to attack, ban, boycott, or prevent the sale of the book. It is highly significant that Mudie's, the leading circulating library, which was often absurdly sensitive about books that offended religious or moral feelings, took five hundred copies, a very large order indeed for them, especially of a nonfiction work—and more than one third of the first edition. That amounts almost to a stamp of approval from society. The churches, and not least the Church of England, were surprisingly uncombative. There was a reason for this, another instance of Darwin's phenomenal good luck. The Church was always much more interested, and ferocious, in waging internal battles over doctrine than in seeking to repel scientific boarders. At the time *Origin* appeared, the conservative element in Anglicanism was gearing itself up for the forthcoming publication of *Essays and Reviews* in 1860, a widely predicted "frontal assault" on orthodoxy by a group of liberal clergymen. This aroused an enormous uproar before, during, and after publication, and a rash of legal actions to deprive the perpetrators of the outrage of their benefices and orders. By comparison, *Origin* slipped through almost unchallenged. There were some critical reviews by the clergy. On the other hand, some clerics were favorable. The Reverend F. J. A. Hunt, prominent as one of the scholars who produced the revision of the New Testament, wrote: "I am inclined to think it unanswerable. In any case it is a treat to read such a book."

No one publicly presented Darwin as an enemy of religion. There is a certain amount of mythology on this point. Part of the myth concerns the meeting of the British Association at Oxford, and the confrontation between T. H. Huxley and Bishop Samuel Wilberforce. The Bishop was not popular in all quarters, being known in the House of Lords as "Soapey Sam" or "the Saponaceous One," among the advanced Whigs and Liberals. Huxley used the occasion for a fight, and the bishop played into his hands by an unfortunate joke about simian ancestry on the paternal or maternal side. Huxley did not like jokes unless he made them himself, and let fly, later spreading the tale that the bishop had been savaged. The bishop thought he himself had won the debate. Others called it a draw. What is true is that FitzRoy made an ass of himself. Now an admiral, he had come to the meeting to read a paper on storms but took the opportunity to protest against the *Origin* by holding up an enormous Bible and begging the audience "to believe God rather than man." He was howled down. A Lady Brewster is said to have fainted—but then, the room was crowded and hot. What is clear is that Wilberforce behaved to all with his customary courtesy, and Huxley with some reluctance conformed. It was a gentlemanly age. Wilberforce reviewed *Origin* in the *Quarterly Review* at enormous length—seventeen thousand words. In many ways, he was complimentary, and the review drew forth from Darwin the remark that it was "uncommonly clever." The bishop met Darwin several times, and his friendly verdict was "He is such a capital fellow." Of course, those who believe the myth that Wilberforce was a dedicated enemy of evolution and *Origin* forget that the Wilberforce family was part of the ramifying network of evangelicals and reformers who had played such an important part in getting through Parliament the original statute banning the slave trade in 1807. The bill was effectively carried by Bishop Wilberforce's father, the MP for Yorkshire, and for people like Emma, the name Wilberforce had a special reverential magic.

The truth is that *Origin* had a surprisingly good press, thanks in part to Darwin's careful avoidance of any statements or phrases that might give offense and to his cultivation of potential reviewers. All his fears proved groundless. Indeed, Emma rejoiced in the book's reception and wrote to their son William at Cambridge: "It is a wonderful thing the whole edition selling off at once & Mudie taking 500 copies." She seems to have taken as much pleasure as Darwin himself in good reviews—a majority of the forty-four that appeared in the first year—and showed her anger at the unfortunate tone of Owen's comments. She was a loyal wife, and her support and evident approval of the book as a work of professional scholarship removed a huge burden from Darwin's shoulders.

As final proof that *Origin* was accepted and there was to be no campaign against him, word came down that Windsor was not hostile to either evolution or natural selection. Whether Queen Victoria read the book is not clear, but she seems to have believed that Prince Albert would have given the book and the theory a fair hearing. When Lyell stayed at Osborne as her guest in 1863 he reported, "[Victoria] asked me a good deal about the Darwin theory as well as the antiquity of man. She has a clear understanding and thinks quite fearlessly for herself, and yet very modestly." Her eldest daughter noted, with approval, "Old opinions have received a shake from which they will never recover." The likelihood is that Queen Victoria would have welcomed an opportunity to meet Darwin as she met Huxley, who left a striking record of his encounter. Charles and Victoria were both fascinated by many aspects of animal life. In 1838 the first orangutan was brought to London and was lodged at the zoo in a special heated giraffe house. Darwin saw this creature, called Jenny, and was particularly fascinated by what he called her "human emotions." When the keeper refused to give her an apple she had seen, "she threw herself on her back, kicked and cried, precisely like a naughty child." The keeper told her: "Jenny, if you will stop barking and be a good girl, I will give you the apple." She understood "every word of this," stopped whining, and got the apple, "with which she jumped into an armchair and began eating it, with the most contented countenance possible." Darwin was so fascinated by Jenny that he invented a phrase, "Go the whole orang," meaning risk offending opponents of evolution by stressing man's descent from apes.

Jenny's successor, another Jenny, likewise intrigued Victoria, who watched her drinking a cup of tea "with horrified fascination at her refined gentility." The queen's conclusion was that the orang was "disagreeably human." She was enthralled when Sir James Paxton showed her his special display of extinct animals in 1858. "What beasts they must have been," she said, "and why did they become extinct?" A year later, Darwin devoted a chapter to this very point and could have expounded on it in person. But the queen may have been put off by Disraeli, who persisted in treating the whole subject of evolution as a subject for mirth. In 1861, attending the Oxford Diocesan Conference, presided over by Wilberforce, Disraeli asked rhetorically, "Is man an ape or an angel? Now, my Lord, I am on the side of the angels." Disraeli never showed any interest in meeting Darwin. Not so his mortal rival, Gladstone, who paid him a friendly call at Down and gave him a two-hour lecture on Turkish atrocities (it was 1878) before remembering to ask him about the future of evolution. Would the future belong to America? Darwin, who had been stunned into silence by the grand old man's verbosity, simply answered, "Yes." When Gladstone left, Darwin said: "What an honour that such a great man should come to visit me." Gladstone made a note in his diary about Darwin's "pleasing and remarkable appearance."

The *Origin* established itself immediately as an "important" book and has remained such ever since. Darwin saw it through five editions and made many corrections. His pride in his own gentlemanly modesty was stung when people reminded him that others besides himself had got on to natural selection. So he changed "my theory" to "the theory" throughout, a total of fifteen times, but missed one "my." To his consternation, he found that the "mathematical expert" who had "worked out the number of elephants that would emerge under Malthusian theory at 15 million" had got his sums wrong, and the figure had to be made less frightening. Not for the first time, he cursed the fact that he could not do math himself.

His correspondence increased enormously. Sedgwick wrote to tell him, sadly, that the book had given him "more pain than pleasure," though "Parts of it I admired greatly, [and] parts I laughed at till my sides were almost sore." (Which parts? One would like to know.) But Sedgwick insisted on putting questions about it in Cambridge exam papers. So, as the publisher, Murray, triumphantly reported, undergraduates had been forced to buy the book. Harriet Martineau exclaimed, "What a book it is. . . . The range & mass of knowledge take away one's breath." John Henslow, though critical of the theory, called it "a marvellous assemblage of facts & observations." Among intellectual potentates who praised it were Henry Buckle, Charles Kingsley, and William Hooker. Among scientists, the vast majority of those under fifty were on Darwin's side, and almost all the under-forties. For the first time, a progressive lobby began to build up in the scientific community. Darwin compiled a list of fifteen distinguished supporters among the geologists, zoologists, paleontologists, physiologists, and botanists. By May he was writing, "If we all stick to it we shall surely gain the day. And I now see that the battle is worth fighting." In fact, Darwin never had to fight a public battle. He did not suffer in the smallest degree professionally as a result of *Origin*. Being sensitive, he was hurt by critical reviews. But that was all. In the not so long run, it was scientists who opposed him who were in danger of victimization. The persecution of Darwin is pure myth. On the contrary, he found himself an eminent Victorian. *Darwinism* became a term circulating in London society. In Germany, *Darwinismus* was hailed enthusiastically as the translation circulated. Indeed the Germans treated him as a hero: In no other country did natural selection, or rather the "survival of the fittest," catch on so fast. Other translations swiftly followed. His ideas were particularly well received in Japan, then just beginning to enter the modern world and industrialize itself. Soon—by the mid-1860s—there was no corner of the earth where Darwin was not known as "the famous scientist."

What should he do now? Lyell and he agreed that he ought to "go the whole orang" and write a book showing in detail how man fitted into evolution and natural selection. That was the logical and satisfying thing to do. It was also what he ought to do, now that it was clear Emma was not upset by the way things were going. But so clear and simple a course was not Darwin's way. He had written *Origin* under a kind of compulsion, because of Wallace. Now he was under no obligation at all, other than his own wishes and scientific concerns. Darwin had twenty-two years to go when *Origin* came out, and he was hard at work, either acquiring facts by observation and experiment or setting them down in orderly form on paper, virtually all the time when not ill. But it is difficult to make logical and categorical sense of his progress. He liked to have several projects going at once and switch from one to another as the spirit or the excitement generated by results moved him—from zoology to botany to physiology or anthropology, from insects to plants, the invertebrates, to men, and back to insects again. That was the trouble with being a polymath, though we must never forget that it was also Darwin's great strength.

The going-the-whole-orang book finally came out in 1871, under the title of *The Descent of Man and Selection in Relation to Sex*. It is a very awkward volume, much longer than *Origin* and far more academic, with plenty of footnotes and source citations, and many line illustrations. But it is a confused and confusing

Paul Johnson

book, quite unlike *Origin* with its single and concentrated argument running throughout. In fact it is two books. The first puts the evolution of man from lower forms into the general context of *Origin*. Indeed, it should have formed part of *Origin* and would have done if Darwin had dared, for he says he had been collecting notes on the subject since the 1830s. But he would never have ventured to proclaim in *Origin* the unqualified assertion that forms the last sentence of *Descent:*

> We must . . . acknowledge . . . that man, with all his noble qualities, with sympathy which feels for the most debased, with benevolence which extends not only to other men but to the humblest living creature, with his godlike intellect which has penetrated into the movements and constitution of the solar system—with all these exalted powers— Man still bears in his bodily frame the indelible stamp of his lowly origin.

However, this argument forms only a part (less than one-third) of the book, and even this is only partly concerned with natural selection on man's evolution. The first chapter covers the "evidence of the Descent of Man from some Lower Form"; the second the "Manner of Development of this descent." Then there are two chapters on comparing the mental powers of men and the "lower animals," followed by three on the evolved man: on his "Intellectual and Moral Faculties during Primeval and Civilised times," on his affinities, and on the "Races of Man." In effect, then, only about sixty pages cover man's evolution from lower forms.

The remaining two thirds of the book deals with the role of sex in natural selection. Darwin had become uneasily aware that natural selection, though generally true, did not cover man comprehensively and would not stand up as the sole explanation. He decided to bolster it by examining the way in which mating is decided by either the male or the female or both. This really should have been a separate book, and the first third should have been added to a new edition of *Origin*. But Darwin did not like to do this, as it would carry the implication that he dodged treating man in the first book, though he already possessed the evidence, such as it was. So the two books were lumped awkwardly together.

There are two further faults in construction. Though the title *Descent of Man* implies that the book is essentially about human beings, of the fourteen chapters dealing with sexual selection, only two concern our species. The last chapter is a general summary and conclusion. Eleven chapters, forming the largest single part of the book, deal with the lower classes of the organic kingdom: insects, butterflies and moths particularly, fishes, amphibians and reptiles, a large section on birds (four chapters), and two chapters on mammals. Here again we have to note Darwin's weakness in anthropology: He simply had much more accurate and convincing information about other species than man, and that was why they occupied much more room. The title of the book as a whole was thus misleading. Second, he had originally intended to include a chapter on emotional expression, containing a lot of material on humans, which would have a little strengthened the claim of the book to be about them. But in the end, he decided to expand the chapter into a separate book, and this was eventually published at the end of the following year, in November 1872, under the title *The Expression of the Emotions in Man and Animals.*

So Darwin's work on evolution through natural selection encompasses three books, not one. And it may be felt that it would have been better if he had published only the first, for it is much superior, as a work of science, to the second and third. The fact is, Darwin had done by far his most original and groundbreaking work on the other forms of organic life, as opposed to man, and he continued to do so till the end of his life. On plants and marine life, on insects, birds, and invertebrates, even to some extent on mammals as a whole, he has a skill and sureness of touch, a knowledge and instinct, even a kind of insightful genius, that eludes him when he comes to man, and the more one reads the trilogy and reflects upon it, the more apparent this discrepancy becomes.

Not that volumes two and three were failures in any way. Certainly not commercially. *The Descent of Man* made two thick volumes selling at £1 4 s., a much bulkier proposition than *Origin*, and more copies printed. But all were sold out in three weeks, and soon 4,500 copies were in print. Darwin made £1,500 immediately, the largest sum he was ever to earn in a lump. *Expressions* had a print run of 7,000 copies and proved highly popular, being on a subject that fascinated the least scientific people and illustrated by photographs of hysterics, lunatics, savages, and other interesting mug shots. Both books also helped substantially to reinforce Darwin's theory that man differed from other animals only in degree, not in kind, which was the real issue once evolution had been accepted. But neither book had the impact of *Origin* among clever and educated people, and *Descent* came in for a good deal of criticism, much of it justified. If either or both had been published without *Origin* preceding them, they might have attracted little attention. And neither could be successfully published today, except on the solid stone bedrock of Darwin's unshakable reputation.

The trouble with *Descent* really starts in chapter 5, "On the Development of the Intellectual and Moral Faculties during Primæval and Civilised Times." It is a mass of generalizations usually unsupported by strict evidence. Much of it was derived from Darwin's friends, the jack-of-all-trades journalist W. R. Greg and his cousin Francis Galton, who was an ingenious compiler of dubious sociological statistics. Greg and Galton examine, for instance, the way in which human folly and improvidence hold back the improving work of natural selection. Thus, "As Mr. Greg puts the case: 'The careless, squalid, unaspiring Irishman multiplies like rabbits: the frugal, farseeing, self-respecting, ambitious Scot, stern in his morality, spiritual in his faith, sagacious and disciplined in his intelligence, passes his best years in struggle and in celibacy, marries late and leaves few behind him.'" Publishing this today would risk prosecution under the hate laws. Even in 1871, it brought a letter of protest from an Irishman, asking Darwin to remove the slur from later editions, but the author flatly refused. There is much to the same effect: "The very poor and reckless, who are often degraded by vice, almost invariably marry early, while the careful and frugal, who are genuinely otherwise virtuous, marry late in life." Darwin makes some odd assertions derived from French figures: "Unmarried men throughout France ... die in a much larger proportion than the married," and "Twice as many wives under twenty die in the year, as died out of the same number of the married." He quotes a Dr. Stark: "Bachelorhood is more destructive to life than the most unwholesome trades, or than residence in an unwholesome house or district. . . ." Stark concludes that lessened mortality is the direct result of marriage. Another of Darwin's odd French sources told him that "civilised man" had been found "whenever compared, to be physically stronger than savages."

Darwin tells us that vaccination works against natural selection, as it "has preserved thousands, who from a weak constitution would formerly have succumbed to smallpox. Thus the weak members of civilised societies propagate their kind." For the same reason, he opposed any form of birth control. When Charles Bradlaugh and Annie Besant were prosecuted for copublishing contraceptive advice and subpoenaed Darwin to give evidence for them, he instantly refused, pleading illness, and said that in any case, he would have to give evidence against them. He quoted *Descent:* "Our natural rate of increase, though leading to many and obvious evils, must not be greatly diminished by any means."

As for moral qualities, he was happy to report in *Descent* that the tendency of the improvident and vicious to breed more than the frugal and virtuous was checked by various factors. "Some elimination of the worst dispositions is always in progress." "Malefactors are executed or imprisoned for long periods. . . ." "Melancholic and insane persons are confined, or commit suicide. Violent and quarrelsome men often come to a bloody end." And so on. This is rambling stuff of no scientific value whatever, the points, even if true, not worth making. It is accompanied by many racial generalizations that now would be denounced as racism or chauvinism. There is a passage, for instance, praising Anglo-Saxon emigration and conquest of lesser breeds—"a nation which produced during a lengthened period the greatest number of highly intellectual, energetic, brave, patriotic and benevolent men, would generally prevail over less favoured nations." He regretted that the principle of natural selection, even so, was not always working powerfully enough, for "we see in many parts of the world enormous areas of the most fertile land capable of supporting numerous happy homes, but peopled only by a few wandering savages." This was the line soon to be taken by Cecil Rhodes, the sort of man, in Darwin's view, required for natural selection to work at its best. As it was, he detected a softening of once valuable forces. In South America, "a people which may be called civilised, such as the Spanish settlers, is liable to become indolent and to retrograde, when the conditions of life are very easy." Selection did not, alas, work so well among such folk, as they "do not supplant and exterminate one another as do savage tribes." He thought progress depended to a great extent on education during youth, "whilst the brain is impressible."

This last point is a reminder that one of Darwin's intellectual weaknesses was to accept the Lamarckian doctrine that acquired characteristics could be inherited, later shown conclusively to be baseless. He thought the lesson applied particularly to women, who should be encouraged to learn things and read widely before they had children, so as to be sure to pass on what they had acquired. One of the points about *Descent* that strikes one particularly today is the evidently low opinion Darwin held of female intelligence, among human beings if not necessarily of insects. This is all the more remarkable in that Emma Darwin was in some ways a wiser person than himself (one might say, in many ways).

He makes the point of superior male intelligence again and again. Man is always "attaining to a higher eminence, in whatever he takes up, than can woman—whether requiring deep thought, reason, or imagination, or merely the use of the senses or hands." Lists of the greatest in poetry, painting, sculpture, or music (composition or performance) would prove this; they "would not bear comparison" and "the average of mental power in man must be above that of women." His source was his cousin Galton's work *Hereditary Genius*. Men have higher energy, perseverance and courage—more patience, too. Both natural and sexual selection reinforced male powers—"Thus, man has ultimately become superior to woman." Then, in an extraordinary sentence, he says it is "fortunate that the law of the equal transmission of characters to both sexes prevails with mammals; otherwise, it is probable that man would have become as superior in mental endowment to woman, as the peacock is in ornamental plumage to the peahen."

Darwin's comments on different races often makes equally painful or hilarious reading. Many Hottentot women, he asserts, are steatopygous—that is, "the posterior part of the body projects in a wonderful manner." He instances the woman "so immensely developed behind that when seated on level ground she could not rise, and had to push herself along until she came to a slope." For this reason she "was considered a beauty."

There are many such anecdotes. Thus: "With the Tahitians, to be called *long-nose* is considered as an insult." From time to time the especially savage Fuegans make their appearance as stage props. And Darwin is especially severe with savages over their sexual habits: "It need hardly be added that, with all savages, female slaves serve as concubines." Certain tribes practice "communal marriages; that is, all the men and women in the tribe are husbands and wives to one another." He adds: "The licentiousness of many savages is no doubt astonishing, but it seems to me that more evidence is requisite." He quotes experts, "whose judgment is worth much more than mine," as believing communal marriage "was the original and universal form throughout the world, including therein the intermarriage of brothers and sisters." One wonders whether Darwin put this sort of information in to titillate or frighten the reader, rather like the imaginary "fifteen million elephants" of *Origin*. He soon follows it with a passage about "capturing wives" as a matter of "honour" also becoming "a universal habit." However, he thinks that "the feeling of jealousy all through the animal kingdom" is so strong that "I cannot believe that absolutely promiscuous intercourse prevailed in times past." His conclusion is that "although savages are now extremely licentious," many tribes "practise some form of marriage, but of a far more lax nature than that of civilised nations." In a footnote, he credits "the Rev. Mr Shooter" to the effect that "the Kafir buy their wives" and "girls are severely beaten by their fathers if they will not accept a chosen husband" but all the same, they have some "power of choice" and "ugly, though rich, men have been known to fail in getting wives." Then he gets on to body hair and skin color, and so to his summary and conclusion. This ends, one is delighted to see, with a final virtuoso performance by the Fuegan, "absolutely naked and bedaubed with paint," a monster "who delights to torture his enemies, offers up bloody sacrifices, practices infanticide without remorse, treats his wives like slaves, knows no decency, and is haunted by the grossest superstitions." He reflects: "Such were our ancestors."

The *Expression of the Emotions* is a much shorter book than *Descent* and took only four months to write, though based on work going back nearly thirty years. It came out in London in November 1872, in America in 1873, and was translated into Russian in 1872, into German, Dutch, and Polish in 1873, French in 1874, and Italian in 1890. As a result of the remarkable boosting of Darwin in recent years, translations have appeared in Chinese in 1996, Spanish in 1998, and Portuguese in 2000. It is, in a way, an essential part of the natural selection trilogy, in that its central argument seems to prove that "some expressions" of men cannot be understood "except on the belief that man once existed in a much lower and animal-like condition." It has a further interest in that Darwin goes to some lengths explaining how he compiled the book by observing infants, by consulting the keepers of insane asylums and experts on "galvanising" (electrotherapy), by looking at large numbers of photos and art prints, and by getting experts all over the world to answer a set of sixteen queries. He goes into some detail about the answers received from those who have studied the Maoris, the Dyaks, the Malays, the Chinese, the Indians, and the Kafirs and Fingoes of Africa. The Fuegans make their usual appearance, as do various tribes from the United States. The photographs are striking, though they give the book a period appearance, as does much of the text.

The best parts of the book by far concern animals: weeping elephants, enraged gorillas, disappointed chimpanzees, terrified cats, grinning dogs, and other phenomena, described by Darwin with the pleasure and skill he always brings to nonhuman behavior and which he finds so difficult to display with man. And his animal anecdotes are more credible than the ones he tells about men and women. The man who vomited when told he had inherited a fortune, "though no odour of alcohol could be detected," the lion tamer whose hair fell out in a single night, and the Indian whose locks precipitately changed from black to white while awaiting execution do not seem very plausible figures; nor do we quite believe Darwin's general assertion that "martyrs, in the ecstasy of their religious fervour," are often "insensible to the most horrid tortures." Sometimes, indeed, one suspects Darwin led a very sheltered existence, as when he asserts, "No poor man would laugh or smile on suddenly hearing that a large fortune had been bequeathed to him." But of course he *did* lead a sheltered existence as a rule, and poor men did not come his way often. He lived among the cultured well-to-do.

By the time *Expression* was published, Darwin had, or thought he had, accomplished his life's work. He had certainly established, to the satisfaction of most educated people, that evolution was a fact, and he had persuaded many of them, albeit still a minority, that evolution embraced all creatures, including man. He had also put across the why of evolution, natural selection, as the general if not exclusive explanation of why it occurred. But he had not discovered exactly, or even vaguely, *how* it operated. We now turn to the great missed opportunity of his crowded and fruitful life.

CHAPTER SIX

How the Great Botanist
Missed an Opportunity

D arwin was a polymath. It was his great strength. Without the breadth as well as the depth of his knowledge, it is doubtful whether *Origin* could have succeeded. But his polymathy was of varying richness and intensity. He switched from one kind of work to another so often in his life and worked on two or three projects simultaneously or intermittently as a matter of habit, so it is not possible, despite his notebooks and diaries, to calculate exactly how much time he spent on each science. But it is likely that more than four fifths of his time went to plants, insects, and small creatures. He loved such work, and he instinctively recognized that he was better at it than at any other form of investigation. He was particularly intrigued when the work involved two branches of study, the interrelationship between insects and plants in the process of fertilization. His son Francis, who wrote his life, says he regarded such study, indulged in when he was supposed to be hard at work on natural selection, as "culpable idleness." In fact, it occupied a good deal of his time, mental energy, and imaginative effort from the late 1830s onward, and after 1872 when he felt he had done his bit on evolution and its dynamics, it became his chief occupation by far.

He started to publish on plant fertilization in 1857–58, when he wrote on the kidney bean for the *Gardeners' Chronicle*. In 1860 he switched to orchids, and after he built his new orchid house at

Down, he devoted six months entirely to the project, finishing in April 1862 the book he called *The Fertilisation of Orchids*. Orchids are beautiful things, and the pleasure Darwin got in finding out their secret history and how insects served them conveys itself to the reader, so it is highly enjoyable even to nongardeners and completely convincing. When Darwin deals with orchids as opposed to "savages," one feels he knows exactly what he is writing about. As a pendant to the orchid book, he worked for eleven years on a technical treatise eventually published in 1876 called *The Effects of Cross and Self Fertilisation in the Vegetable Kingdom*. His son Francis says that the whole project arose out of an accidental observation. Darwin had very sharp eyes, as photographs suggest, and he loved to pounce on and dig into anything unusual, even if the visual registration did not ring a bell to his mind for two or three days (as with Fleming's discovery of penicillin). In this case, the unusual happened twice before he noticed it, and that was uncharacteristic but made the eventual double take all the more sharp and satisfying.

He next moved on to the details of the sexual life of plants, especially primroses, and if Disraeli had known this, he might have taken Darwin more seriously, for the primrose was his favorite flower, and he grew masses of splendid varieties at Hughenden. Darwin said he got more pleasure out of this research than anything else he did, and he learned a lot about plant hermaphrodites, heterocycles, hybridization, and infertility. He published a paper on this in 1863 but went on working at it, and a book, *The Different Forms of Flowers on Plants of the Same Species*, appeared in 1877. He also got a great deal of pleasure from studying climbing plants and worked out in enormous detail exactly why and how they climbed, what and when, and the consequences. Simultaneously he worked on insectivorous plants, and he got very excited about the way in which vegetation, in moving purposefully and attacking insect prey, behaves almost like animals. These investigations produced two books, *Insectivorous Plants* (1876) and *The Power of Movement in Plants* (1880). The latter was a formidable work: over six hundred pages and nearly two hundred illustrations.

Darwin loved working on plants because he had everything necessary at hand: greenhouses, special hothouse areas, ample soil for plantings, gardeners to assist, and notes going back forty years. He also had children, and later grandchildren, of various ages to perform special tasks. Plants led to his last object of inquiry into invertebrates: worms. Here again, he had been interested in worms for the best part of half a century, and in his last years, they occupied his mind more than any other aspect of nature. He had published a paper on worms for the Geological Society journal in 1838. Now he tied up worms with botany by working on a book called *The Formation of Vegetable Mould, Through the Action of Worms, with Observations on Their Habits.* He wrote: "This is a subject of but small importance; and I know not whether it will interest many readers. But it has interested me." In fact, to visit Down House during the worm years, one would have thought no more important creature ever existed. Large parts of the garden were devoted to producing, nourishing, and classifying worms. The billiard room was made into a worm sanctuary. The billiard table itself was covered in pots with glass tops wherein particularly important worms were kept for observation. The entire family was made worm conscious. Darwin wanted to know everything about worms: their sense of touch, their appetites, their hearing, eyesight, and emotions. He would get up at night, pad downstairs in his nightshirt, and flash paraffin lamps at them. He used oil lamps, too, matches, candles, and "dark" lanterns, which he equipped with various colored slides. He experimented with endless kinds of food, from minced meat to fish paste. They would not eat bread or cheese or apples. What they liked were greens, especially cabbage. They loved carrots. He got Emma to play the piano to them, but they took no notice. They failed to respond to firecrackers, children's percussion caps, or sparklers. His son Frank played his bassoon, and another son, Bernard, blew a tin whistle. Nothing. His daughter Bessy sang and called out loud: "Worms! Worms!" Again, no response. Darwin found they would try to get away from bright lights and slither underground. But they were not interested in a red-hot poker held nearby. He discovered they liked touching each other, and their sexuality was stronger than their aversion to strong light. They obviously enjoyed their food. He thought that they could acquire a notion of an object by touching it in many places. They could, he argued, solve problems. They were rather like a man "born blind and deaf." Thus, once again, he proved, at least to his own satisfaction, that the difference between human beings and lowly organisms was not as great as people thought. Worms, like barnacles, could think, in their own way. The book proved surprisingly popular, and Darwin enormously enjoyed the entire project, even including the writing.

In fact it is likely that Darwin's botanical and quasi-botanical studies such as worms were the most pleasurable part of his entire work. He was a better botanist than anything else. This makes it all the more tragic that he never became aware of the importance of the work being done by the greatest botanist of his time, perhaps of all time, Gregor Mendel.

He was thirteen years younger than Darwin, born in 1822 in Austria but spending his scientific life in Brünn, now Brno in the Czech Republic. His father was a farmer, and Mendel acquired his love of plants in the orchard, gardens, and fields of his father's farm. After a mixed academic career, he became an Augustinian monk (like Luther) in 1843 and was ordained a priest four years later. Able and well organized, he rose to be abbot of his monastery. He began working and experimenting in the monastery garden in 1856. The monks loved fresh peas, and Mendel tried to produce new and more nourishing and delightful varieties. The monastery and the school where he taught had good scientific libraries, which took in foreign publications: Mendel possessed both the *Origin* and the *Descent*, writing notes in the margin, and was familiar with the *Gardeners' Journal*. But he was aware of most of the principles of heredity before he read Darwin. He described his specialty as "plant hybridization" and determined to find out everything about it himself. In short he was a man after Darwin's own heart. There was one difference, though. Mendel was a natural mathematician and early grasped the importance of statistics in working out hereditary processes.

Mendel and some scientific-minded friends, early in the 1860s, formed the Natural Science Society of Brünn, which from

1862 began to publish its own journal. In two meetings in February and March 1865, he told the society that all previous attempts to discover the principles of hybridization had been misconceived:

> Not one has been carried out on a scale and manner as to find exactly the number of forms under which the offspring of hybrids appear, or to arrange these forms in exact order according to their different generations, or to discover exactly what are their statistical relationships.

Mendel dismissed existing work on heredity as amateurish and formulated his own, new rules using his pea plantings and blendings as the master guide. He studied particularly color in the blossoms and axils of the leaves, the varying size of the plants at particular points in their growth, and the color, size, and shape of the seeds. He also noted the position of flowers on the stem and the placing of the pods. He discovered that significant variations in all the visible alternatives were due to the pairing of what he concluded were the elementary units of heredity—what we would call genes. He realized that these basic units obey comparatively simple statistical laws and that such laws apply to all organic species, including human beings. Mendel's first law, as it is now known, is that the reproductive cells of the hybrids are always divided into two groups: half transmit one parental unit, and half the other. This *principle of segregation* explains why it is possible to predict exactly what happens when single pairs of alternative characteristics operate through a number of generations. He discovered that when several pairs of alternative traits are studied, these several pairs are transmitted to the progeny in all the possible combinations. He pinpointed seven pairs of different traits in his garden pea varieties, recombined them at random on paper according to another law, the *principle of independent assortment*, and worked out mathematically the statistical consequences of what he was doing. Then he confirmed the figures by experiment with real pea varieties. His various hypotheses were shown to be entirely valid, even though we now know that independent assortment operates as a law only in certain conditions. Nevertheless, the general thrust of his work proved valid as one of the fundamental laws of nature. He had, in short, discovered *how* natural selection, or indeed any form of selection, worked. Thus he had completed Darwin's work on evolution, and in a manner that would have appealed strongly to Darwin's tastes and favorite methodologies—by careful practical work in a comparatively small garden using a common plant. Darwin could have done exactly the same at Down. The mathematics might have presented a problem, but not an insuperable one.

Mendel's theory and laws, which laid the foundation of the entirely new science of genetics, and the experiments that led to them were described by Mendel in two papers presented to the Brünn Natural Science Society in 1865 and published in full in the transactions of the society in 1866, in a single long article, "Experiments with Plant Hybrids." This publication was by no means as obscure as it may sound, as it was taken by the major libraries in England, Europe, and America and seen by leading botanists. It is not clear whether Darwin saw a copy of this issue. There is a story that one was found in his library after his death with the pages uncut. This seems to be untrue. But Darwin recommended to a scientific friend a book by Wilhelm Olbers Focke, which mentions the article no less than fourteen times. It is a thousand pities that Mendel did not send his papers directly to Darwin and explain how his work fitted into Darwin's *Origin*. He might so easily have done so, and Darwin, who was always considerate and conscientious in handling foreign scientific correspondents, even if unknown to him, would have responded. As it was, Mendel tried to open a correspondence with a leading German botanist, Professor Karl Wilhelm von Nägeli of Munich, but the German turned out to be a blockhead who could follow neither the mathematics nor the logic of the argument. Darwin would have made more effort and gotten the point. The missed opportunity is of the greatest importance, for in 1866 Darwin had a decade and a half of good work ahead of him. If he had been apprised of genetic theory then, he could have entered a new world of discovery. *The Descent of Man* had not yet been written and would have been totally different and much better if Darwin had been able to give the how as well as the why of natural selection. The truth is, he did not always use his ample financial resources to the best effect. He might build new greenhouses and recruit an extra gardener or two, but he held back on employing trained scientific assistants. A young man with language and mathematical skills, with specific instructions to comb through foreign scientific publications for news of work relevant to Darwin's particular interest, would have been invaluable to him. Such an assistant would almost certainly have drawn his attention to Mendel's work and given him a digest in English. There is no question that Darwin could have afforded such help. During these years he was regularly showing a large surplus on his accounts, and reinvesting up to £5,000 a year. But his old fears about being attacked by religious fanatics—the shadow of Priestley—appear to have been succeeded by equally baseless fears of losing his money and going bankrupt. Indeed at one point, he even made enquiries about Australia as a safer place to live and invest his capital, so he saved when he should have spent. Darwin and Mendel, two of the greatest scientists of the epoch, never came into contact.

Mendel was in some ways a more thorough scientist than Darwin. Though he worked on a much narrower front, the scale of his experiments was greater by far. Darwin believed, quite wrongly, that inheritance was a blend. Mendel discovered that there was no mingling. The characteristics did not mix. One is dominant, the other recessive. Of nearly 20,000 hybrid pea plants of the second generation—19,959 to be exact—Mendel, by counting them himself with infinite care, found that the dominants outnumbered the recessives by 14,949 to 5,010, or nearly three to one. The hybrid carried the imprint of either one parent or the other, but not of both. If the inheritance blended, like a mixture of two fluids, then natural selection would not work, because the new and improved hybrid would be lost in the process by which descent diluted the inheritance. Curiously enough, a Scotsman, Fleeming Jenkin, had noticed this, arguing that inheritance based on blends would defeat the whole principle of natural selection. He attacked Darwin accordingly. Darwin was clearly worried by this line of argument and seems to have retreated from the blending idea. He wrote to Huxley, "I have lately been inclined to speculate, very crudely and indistinctly, that propagation by true fertilisation will turn out to be a sort of mixture, and not true fusion, of two distinct individuals. [That was why] crossed forms go back to so large an extent to ancestral forms." If Darwin had followed this line of thought, he might have reached the same conclusions as Mendel independently. Instead he spent the last, precious years of his life on climbing plants and earthworms and plants that swallow insects. All useful and commendable stuff and clearly delightful to him, but not the material from which dramatic scientific progress emerged. One has the feeling that Darwin was often inclined to avoid the hard cerebral activity of thinking through fundamental scientific principles, taking comfortable refuge in minute observations. So his work on species remained incomplete.

As for Mendel, he outlived Darwin by nearly two years but never got any recognition of his genius. In 1868 he was made abbot of his monastery, the rest of his life was spent largely in administration, and his work passed into limbo. Only in 1900, when he and Darwin had been dead nearly two decades, did three European botanists quite independently develop the same ideas about inheritance. They then, in searching the literature, came across Mendel's papers, and realized the importance of his work. The science of genetics then began in earnest, and Mendel got due credit. But the blending of Darwin and Mendel never took place. Instead there was a new hybrid, a true monster—social Darwinism in its various forms.

CHAPTER SEVEN

Evils of Social Darwinism

Darwin's later years were ones of growing fame and personal celebrity but of decreasing happiness. Having missed a grand opportunity of discovering genetics, he came to recognize that the work he was doing was somehow unsatisfactory. He wrote to Hooker, "I am rather despondent about myself." He complained of illness and discomfort, but chiefly of inability to embark on a major project. "I have not the heart or strength at my age to begin any investigation lasting years, which is the only thing which I enjoy, & I have no little jobs which I can do." He admitted that "I have everything to make me happy and contented, but life has become very wearisome to me." He was also perturbed by the ever wider and adventurous use thinkers at home and abroad were making of his work on evolution, for political, economic, and ideological purposes. He found himself under the lengthening shadow of social Darwinism.

The *Origin* had an enormous and rapid impact on the investigation of almost all human activities. Those who studied progress were hugely attracted by Darwin's notion of natural selection as a relentless, self-directing machine, "daily and hourly scrutinising, throughout the world, every variation . . . silently and insensibly working . . . at the improvement of each organic being. . . ." Darwin's words caused lip-smacking delight among writers and intellectuals. They also loved his presentation of organic life as a ferocious drama of "struggle" and "survival," the two key words, which soon occupied a prominent place in every tract of the times. Herbert Spencer, the archetypal polymath and guru, who had got on to "the survival of the fittest" even before Darwin, received a dynamic boost from the universal success of *Origin* and was delighted to see the great scientist adopt his phrase.

Spencer enlarged the debate in two ways. First, the struggle to survive applied not just to individuals but to entire societies and nations. Second, evolution provided an explanation for all phenomena—political, economic, military, psychological, and social. He admitted that a "final explanation" was not possible. That depended on the "Ultimate Cause," what he called "The Unknowable." That apart, all could be worked out, and starting in 1860, the year after *Origin,* he gradually produced his enormous *System of Synthetic Philosophy,* at last finished in 1896. In 1872, just after Darwin produced *Descent,* Spencer was joined by another highly representative guru, Walter Bagehot, *Economist* editor and author of the classic work on the English constitution, who has been described as the "greatest Victorian." His *Physics and Politics; or, Thoughts on the Application of the Principles of "Natural Selection" and "Inheritance" to Political Society* was an analysis of English history and current leadership in the world in terms of Darwinian evolution. Though Spencer and Bagehot saw England going ever upward, like Darwin's man, they warned of dangers in the continuing struggle, with the lower classes seen rather like the primitive savages from whom the progressive middle class had triumphantly evolved, now threatening regressive antiprogress by revolution, violence, and all-out democracy. Darwin's work also inspired the fear that top nations like Britain might become degenerate by dilution of its racial purity. Charles Kingsley warned that "physical science is proving more and more the immense importance of Race, the importance of hereditary powers, hereditary organs, hereditary habits, in all organised beings, from the lowest plant to the highest animal." The racial or "favoured nation" theory of history, springing from Darwin, found powerful expression in *The Expansion of England* (1882) by John Robert Seeley, Regius Professor of Modern History at Cambridge, and in James Anthony Froude's *Oceana; or, England and Her Colonies* (1885), Benjamin Kidd's *Social Evolution* (1894), and J. A. Cramb's *Origins and Destiny of Imperial Britain* (1900), all of them big-selling books taken seriously by the educated, ruling class. Lord Rosebery, prime minister from 1894 to 1895, said the English race had a moral duty to "peg out claims for the future" and "it is part of our heritage to take care that the world . . . shall receive an English-speaking complexion, and not that of other nations."

Darwin's writings led directly to the state of mind that promoted imperialism, the quest for colonies, the "race for Africa," and, to use Rhodes's expression, "painting the map of the world red." In less than twenty years, Britain acquired 3.5 million square miles of colonies and a further 1.5 million of protectorates. But of course other nations began to seize colonies too, and expand their earth space, developing their own master-race theories in justification—the Russians, the French, the Japanese, a newcomer to modernity but immensely proud of its undoubted "racial purity," and above all, the Germans. The leading Darwinian historian in Germany, Heinrich von Treitschke, elaborated a fierce racial analysis of Germany's history and triumphant future, and Bismarck started a national program of German imperialism with a slogan of Darwinian resonance, "Blood and Iron."

There was also a drive to improve the racial stock by positive and negative measures. Darwin was always nervous about speculating on the operations of natural selection in the present and was confused about whether society should assist its forces or impede them. He seems to have been opposed to vaccination and other medical processes, which preserved the lines of "weaker" humans. And he explicitly opposed birth control. Despite his hatred of cruelty, he saw the reduction or even extinction of aboriginals in Argentina, New Zealand, and Australia by "the stronger races" as natural and therefore welcome, and he took it for granted that whites would eventually rule Africa and replace the natives. It is vital to remember that in Darwin's lifetime, white European birthrates were historically the highest ever. So Darwin looked on benevolently while the processes of natural selection operated in favor of a world ruled by whites of European origin. But he did not necessarily back any positive measures to help the process of keeping whites "superior" as a race.

His cousin, Francis Galton, had no such inhibitions. The publication of *Origin* was the formative event in his life, and from absorbing its lessons he went on to invent his own science, which he eventually (1885) called eugenics. He began work on a book called *Hereditary Genius* (1869), which argued that civilization, though desirable in itself and proof of the importance of human stock of high mental and physical capabilities, had the unfortunate tendency to increase the number of "unfit" people by preventing

nature from eliminating the weak, mentally ill, and other undesirables. He called the present situation in the 1860s "a sort of intellectual anarchy" for "the want of master-minds." It was no use, he
argued, improving the environment by factory laws, good sanita-
tion, poor laws, and hospitals if the state did nothing to assist the
birth of those with superior minds and bodies and prevent the
birth of the weak. He wanted the state to compile a national bio-
graphical index of "desirables" and "undesirables," and permit
marriage only of those who could produce a certificate of their fit-
ness. Galton, unlike his cousin, was good at math and statistics
and recruited as a follower a first-class statistical innovator named
Karl Pearson, who was terrified by the advancing economic power
of Germany and wanted to combat it by a national program of
selective breeding. Adopting Galton's neologism, he invented the
term "eugenic marriage" and argued that the state should make
unlawful any union that did not qualify.

It is common among Darwin's more enthusiastic scientific followers in the twentieth and twenty-first centuries, who attribute
to their idol powers of prescience and wisdom he clearly did not
possess and would never have dreamed of claiming, to insist that
Darwin had nothing to do with any kind of social Darwinism, let
alone eugenics. He was in no way responsible, they claim, for any
ultimately malign or disastrous consequences of his work on natural selection. This needs qualifying. Darwin was always careful
to steer clear of politics as such. Though by family background
and gentle inclination a Whig or Liberal, he was never a party
man. But he took up some public postures, as his views on vaccination and birth control indicated. He gave broad approval to his

cousin Galton's work. He praised his book warmly on its publication. He drew attention to his work repeatedly and approvingly in both *Descent* and *Expression*. He might have disapproved or even publicly rejected views held after his death by Galton and his followers, but this is pure conjecture. There is nothing to suggest that Darwin was opposed to eugenics in either its positive or its negative practices. Darwin took it as axiomatic that the improvement of the human race, by natural or artificial means, was and is desirable.

Moreover, although Darwin often in theory took up a detached scientific viewpoint, this is constantly belied by his vocabulary, phraseology, and verbal coloring. The actual title of *Origin*, it has been pointed out, uses words like *selection, struggle, favored,* and *preservation,* which imply a mind or force or something more conscious than blind nature at work. *Origin* and *Descent* are dotted with words and phrases that imply design, purpose, or creative intelligence. One critic has noted his fondness for popular phrases like "handsome is as handsome does," "many a mickle makes a muckle," "in the midst of life we are in death," and "the race being to the swift"—as though Mother Nature, far from being impersonal and neuter, was a lady with a taste for proverbs and even for the Bible. Darwin's immediate followers were even less careful in using loaded expressions. Michael Foster, the leading Cambridge physiologist, wrote of nature making "wise and unwise investments in the animal economy," and mammals "living up to their physiological incomes."

The truth is, *Origin* is a book that, with total success,

embodies an exciting idea and had a devastating intellectual and emotional impact on world society. The word *devastating* is accurate: It destroyed many comfortable assumptions, thus clearing space for new concepts and ideas to spring up in almost every subject. It acted like a force of nature itself, and by the end of January 1860, when the second edition sold out, it was quite beyond Darwin's control. Darwin became one of the formative thinkers of the twentieth century, alongside Marx, Freud, and Einstein, affecting the way people thought about an immense variety of topics, often quite remote from his own preoccupations.

Social Darwinism took many forms. Eugenics, as a science, enjoyed only limited success in that national registers of marriageable persons were not compiled and no country insisted on eugenic certificates before allowing a marriage, as Galton had wished. But its companion science, or pseudoscience, of dysgenics, the elimination of the unhealthy, made startling progress for half a century. In 1904 Charles Davenport, a follower of Galton and of Darwin, got the billionaire Andrew Carnegie, a superb example of Samuel Smiles's *Self-Help*, to finance the Cold Spring Harbor Laboratory. This quickly took on board the new science of Mendelism to reinforce Darwinism and preach the doctrine that physical weakness and, still more, mental illness, was inherited, and to lobby state and federal governments to pass laws preventing it. This cause was assisted by concern over immigration and the risk that lower-race arrivals from eastern Europe, especially Jews, would "contaminate" and "weaken" the Anglo-Saxon racial stock of the United States. The passage of the Immigration

Restriction Act of 1924 can be traced back to the publication of the *Origin*. But individual states went further and passed laws giving the authorities the right to sterilize the mentally unfit and certain types of criminals. By 1920 fifteen states had sterilization laws. The U.S. Supreme Court ruled most of them unconstitutional until 1927, when in *Buck v. Bell*, it decided that Virginia could sterilize Carrie Buck, a feeble-minded epileptic, daughter of another low-mentality woman and already the mother of a child judged "an imbecile." Passing judgement, Justice Oliver Wendell Holmes ruled, "Three generations of imbeciles are enough." In the quarter century up to 1935, U.S. states passed over a hundred sterilization laws and sterilized over a hundred thousand people with subnormal mental faculties. Virginia went on sterilizing up to the 1970s.

It is curious that, although sterilization has been practiced on a large scale all over the world, especially in Scandinavia, no investigation has been made to discover whether national dysgenic programs have had any statistically discernible effect on societies. Norway, Finland, Sweden, Iceland, and Estonia all passed laws, and Sweden actually sterilized 65,000 people, a much higher proportion, per capita, than the United States. Except for Canada, the British Empire rejected sterilization, thanks largely to a vigorous campaign conducted by G. K. Chesterton, who wrote a fierce book on the subject. He was helped by a brilliant satire written by Aldous Huxley in 1932, *Brave New World*, which pictured a "dark Utopia" in which science was used in innumerable ways to create a hygienically perfect but docile and submissive population. This combined an attack on Galtonism with a reprise of George Eliot's worry that Darwinian natural selection was a dangerous form of determinism, which would extinguish free will and the human instinct for freedom. It was also a sally against the bright utopia preached by H. G. Wells, in which science was king. Wells, Shaw, Beatrice and Sydney Webb, Havelock Ellis, and many other socialist intellectuals favored both eugenics and dysgenics and would have condemned to sterilization or even death all the mentally unfit if they could have brought to power a government to their taste. But they never persuaded the British Labour Party to adopt their views.

Eugenics became a central plank of national policy in Germany. That is not surprising. Darwin's work was adopted enthusiastically in German scientific circles from the early 1860s on, and *Darwinismus* formed the basis for scientific race theory. Germany became the home for race theorists, such as Houston Stewart Chamberlain, author of an enormous race history of the modern world centered on Germany, who adopted German citizenship in 1916 at the height of the First World War. He emphasized the cultural side of the Aryan master race (as he called it) by living in Bayreuth and marrying Wagner's only daughter, Eva. He held that "so long as there are true *Germanen* in the world so long can and will we have confidence in the future of the human family." But the entrance of the Jews into European history was the intrusion of "an element foreign to everything that Europe had hitherto been, and achieved."

Darwin used phrases like "as rich as Jews" and blamed "a primitive Jewish God" for much that was wrong with Judeo-Christianity, especially the doctrine of eternal punishment, which he thought positively evil. But he was not anti-Semitic. What made his teaching so destructive in Germany was his emphasis on the constant violence involved in natural selection. It is doubtful if Adolf Hitler actually read the *Origin*, but he certainly absorbed its arguments and the psychology of strife seen as necessary for the emergence of higher forms. Hitler was fond of dwelling on the awful prospect (which Thomas Carlyle had made into a joke) of mankind evolving backward or downward. He said:

> If we do not respect the law of nature, imposing our will by the might of the stronger, a day will come when the wild animals will again devour us – when the insects will eat the wild animals, and finally nothing will exist except the microbes. By means of the struggle the elites are continually renewed. The law of selection justifies this incessant struggle by allowing the survival of the fittest. Christianity is a rebellion against natural law, a protest against nature.

Thus we see how ideas develop their own self-sustaining and often destructive careers in history. The emotional stew that built up inside Darwin's mind from seeing the Fuegans, looking at beaks in the Galápagos, and reading Malthus—a stew that permeated with its verbal odors almost every page of *Origin*—became for some a vicious poison. Darwin's fondness for the word *struggle*—he used it dozens of times—was particularly unfortunate. Hitler adopted it and made it the title of his book, which was both autobiography and political program, *Mein Kampf.* Struggle was healthy; it was nature's way. And under the cover and darkness of war, it became easy to resort to another much-used word of Darwin's, *extermination.*

Once in power, Hitler began a process that carried dysgenics to its logical conclusion. Over four hundred thousand mentally unfit persons were sterilized in Nazi Germany between 1933 and 1939. When war came, seventy thousand of these unfortunates, though incapable of breeding, were "exterminated." These mass-extermination programs were the model for the elimination of entire races, gypsies and Jews, with the Slavs to follow if the war lasted long enough. It is important to note that Hitler was not a solitary figure in his peculiar version of *Darwinismus.* In his ascent to power, he always polled better among the university population, professors and students, than among the German electorate as a whole. German biologists who held academic status were almost unanimously behind the eugenics program, and over 50 percent of them were members of the Nazi party, the highest percentage in any professional group. Both Himmler, head of the SS, and Goebbels, the propaganda chief, were students of Darwin.

In the first half of the twentieth century, the notion of struggle being natural and essential in the improvement of humanity was a belief that ran right across the political spectrum. The delight with which Engels and Marx pounced upon the *Origin* the week of its appearance was succeeded by a continuing interest among leading Communists, from Lenin and Trotsky to Stalin and Mao Tse-tung, in Darwin's theory of natural selection as justification for the class struggle. It was essential to the self-respect of Communists to believe that their ideology was scientific, and Darwin provided stiffening to the scaffold of laws and dialectic they erected around their seizure and retention of power. Stalin had Darwin's "struggle" and "survival of the fittest" in mind when dealing with the Kulaks and when relocating the minorities of Greater Russia: extermination of groups was a natural event if the party, redefined as the elite of the politically "fit," was to survive. Mao Tse-tung, who had his own view of Darwin, saw the "struggle" in terms of his Cultural Revolution, in which one embodiment of Communist culture replaced an outmoded and unfit predecessor. Pol Pot, introduced by his professor Jean-Paul Sartre to the idea of evolution to higher forms, translated the theory in terms of Cambodia into an urban-rural struggle in which one fourth of the population died. In the twentieth century, it is likely that over 100 million people were killed or starved to death as a result of totalitarian regimes infected with varieties of social Darwinism. But then Darwin himself had always insisted on the high percentage of destruction involved in breeding, whether of seeds, embryos, births, of even mature birds, mammals, and species in general. Nature, he believed, is always profuse, in death as well as life, and if he had been asked to reflect on the human toll of "struggle" in the twentieth century, he would certainly have pointed out that the world population nevertheless dramatically increased throughout the period. At the time *Origin* was published, there were about 1,325 million human beings in the world. By the time Mao Tse-tung, last of the great "exterminators," died—having himself presided over the deaths of 70 million—the human total had risen to 3,900 million.

CHAPTER EIGHT

Triumph and the Reversal of Natural Selection

F ew men have lived such a successful and contented life as Darwin. The *Origin* was one of those books that established itself immediately and has never been ousted from its salient place in scientific literature. The acclaim for his work culminated in the autumn of 1877, when he was made an honorary doctor of laws at a special meeting of his old university, Cambridge. Emma in a letter to her son William described the scene in the Senate House:

Gallery crammed to overflowing w. Undergraduates & the Floor crammed too w. Undergs. climbing on the statues & standing up in the windows. There seemed to be periodic cheering in answer to jokes which sounded deafening. But when Father came in in his red cloak ushered in by some authorities, it was perfectly deafening for some minutes. I thought he would be overcome but he was quite stout & smiling & sat waiting for the Vice-Chancellor. The time was filled up with shouts & jokes & groans . . . we had been watching some cords stretched across from one gallery to another, wondering what was to happen but we were not surprised to see a monkey dangling down, which caused shouts & jokes about our ancestors etc. Then came a sort of ring tied with ribbons wh. we conjectured to be the "Missing Link." . . . a few Latin words & then it was over & everybody came up & shook hands.

The fact that everyone joked about Darwin and that he liked the jokes endeared him to the public. *Punch* turned him into a familiar figure. When he died, the public demanded that he be buried at Westminster Abbey, and his coffin was borne by ten eminent men: the Dukes of Devonshire and Argyll, the Earl of Derby, the American Ambassador James Russell Lowell, Canon Farrar, and five scientists, Hooker, Huxley, Wallace, John Lubbock, and William Spottiswoode. The *Times* devoted a column and a half to the ceremony, one of the defining funerals of the late Victorian epoch.

Darwin's private life was outwardly happy and placid, underlining his persistent good fortune. Emma was a wise and loving wife and long survived him. Seven of his ten children survived and prospered, George becoming professor of astronomy at Cambridge and winning a knighthood, Francis and Horace being elected fellows of the Royal Society. His many grandchildren delighted him. His finances flourished, and he was able to assist all his progeny to lead comfortable lives. He was esteemed by his neighbors and revered by his servants. Many cherished animals were buried in the gardens, alongside the orchid house, the greenhouse where the plants climbed and devoured insects, and the soggy place where the worms bred.

In his last years, he wrote a good deal of autobiographical material, some of which has survived. It is guarded, though there are occasional flashes of frankness. Thus, when a child: "I was much given to inventing deliberate falsehoods"; "once as a very little boy I acted cruelly, for I beat a puppy, I believe, simply from enjoying the sense of power." He said he was considered by the masters "rather below the common standard in intellect." He quotes his father: "You care for nothing but shooting, dogs & rat-catching, & you will be a disgrace to yourself & all your family." Most of it is anodyne rambling. "I did not care much about the general public. . . . I am sure that I have never turned one inch out of my course to gain fame." "I gradually came to disbelieve in Christianity as a divine revelation"; "The plain language of the [biblical] text seems to show that the men who do not believe, & this would include my Father, Brother & almost all my best friends, will be everlastingly punished. And this is a damnable doctrine." "Few persons can have lived a life more retired than [my wife and I] have done." "[Emma] has been my greatest blessing, & I can declare that in my whole life I have never heard her utter one word which I would rather have been unsaid."

What is the most striking admission is the collapse of his entire cultural life in middle and old age. He lost all interest in art. It is significant that his attempt to get material for his *Expressions* from painting and prints was a failure. On holiday in the Lake District in 1879, the Darwins called on Ruskin at his house overlooking Coniston Lake, and Ruskin showed them his magnificent watercolors by Turner. Darwin took no interest—could see nothing in them. The incomprehension was reciprocated; Ruskin thought Darwin's views on evolution were "pernicious nonsense" and that "if he would get different kinds of air & bottle them, and examine them when bottled, he would do much more useful work than he does in the contemplation of the hinder parts of monkeys." Darwin once got "intense pleasure" from listening to music, though "utterly destitute of an ear [so that] I cannot perceive a discord or keep tune & hum a tune correctly." Later he lost completely whatever taste for music he ever had, and when Emma played, he watched her for the pleasure of admiring the skill as her hands moved over the keys, not for the sounds she produced. He took no interest, for instance, in the great Wagner boom, despite the fact that his work was read to each other by Richard and Cosima Wagner, just as George Eliot and Lewes had done, and despite the reiterated theme of transformation in the operas. Most surprising of all was the disappearance of his taste for poetry. Once, Milton, Byron, Wordsworth, Coleridge, and Shelley "gave me great pleasure" and "I took intense delight in Shakespeare." But he confessed in 1876 that "now for many years I cannot endure to read a line of poetry," and an effort to return to Shakespeare "nauseated me." Even "fine scenery" did not "cause me the exquisite delight" it once did. All he liked was to have read to him novels, "if they do not end unhappily." He did not require high quality, just a character "whom one can thoroughly love, & if it be a pretty woman all the better." Darwin is an archetypal figure in Eliot's *Middlemarch* and Elizabeth Gaskell's *Wives and Daughters*, and the Darwinian impulse is strong in Conrad and Hardy, and still more in Ibsen's plays, where the doom of heredity is a recurring theme. But there is no evidence that Darwin took any interest in the evolution of literature. It is worth repeating his complaint: "My mind seems to have become a kind of machine for grinding general laws, out of large collections of facts." He thought he should have "made a rule to read some poetry & to listen to some music at least once every week," to "keep active through use" those "parts of my brain now atrophied."

He tried as honestly as he could to analyze his own gifts— and shortcomings. "I have no great quickness of apprehension or wit," like Huxley. He thought himself "a poor critic." His power to follow an abstract train of thought was "very limited." His memory was "hazy." But "I am superior to the common run of men in noticing things . . . [and] observing them carefully." He thought his industry was "great," his love of science "steady and ardent." He had, he thought, "patience" and originality, springing from "the ambition to be esteemed by my fellow naturalists." His habits were "methodical," and ill health had "saved me from the distraction of society and amusements." He had enjoyed "a fair share of invention as well as of common sense." However, he was inclined to call his abilities "moderate" and added, "My work has been over and over again greatly overpraised."

It should be noted that Darwin's sharply critical estimate of his own gifts and work was accompanied by often ruthless reflections on his contemporaries. These were for his private eye only: It was against his lifelong practice of networking to disparage fellow savants in public. But his secret thoughts were unedifying. Even Humboldt was a "disappointment," who "talked much." Buckle, too, was "a great talker" who "left no gaps" for others to put a word in. And "I doubt whether his generalisations are worth anything." Spencer was the same—not "of any strictly scientific use" and certainly "no use to me." And "he was extremely egotistical." Owen was "my bitter enemy," inspired by jealousy. He quotes Falconer's opinion that he was "not only ambitious, very envious & arrogant, but untruthful and dishonest." His "power of hatred was certainly unsurpassed." The botanist Robert Brown would not lend plants—"he was a complete miser & knew himself to be a miser." He thought it "a pity" that Huxley had "attacked so many scientific men," albeit he had "worked well for the good of mankind." Hooker was "the most untirable worker I have ever seen" but "very impulsive & somewhat peppery in temper." Herschel's every word was "worth listening to" but when he came into a room, it was "as if he knew his hands were dirty, & that he knew that his wife knew that they were dirty." William Buckland was "vulgar and [an] almost coarse man." The degree to which geologist Roderick Murchison "valued rank was ludicrous." This was the trouble with Lyell too: "very fond of society, especially of eminent men & of persons high in rank." Babbage was "a disappointed & discontented man . . . morose." He quoted him saying, "There is only one thing I hate more than piety, & that is patriotism." He accused Carlyle of "haranguing during the whole of dinner on the advantages of silence," and said of him, "I never met a man with a mind so ill-adapted for scientific research."

In his old age Darwin admitted, "I have lost the power of becoming deeply attached to anyone." He assured Tennyson that there was nothing in his theories to prevent anyone believing in a supreme being. But he did not think about God or the possibility of an afterlife. He closed his mind to speculation about the infinite and concentrated on worms. One is tempted to feel that he deliberately shut his eyes to the ultimate consequences of his work, in terms of the human condition and the purpose of life or the absence of one. Though he sometimes, in his published works, put in a reassuring phrase, his private views tended to be bleak. He wrote to Hooker: "What a book a devil's chaplain might write on the clumsy, wasteful, blundering, low and horribly cruel works of nature." He was always confused about cruelty. In his traveling days, he condemned "buccaneers" and "whalers" for "always taking cruel delight in knocking down the little birds." He thought that "the natives" were cruel in their treatment of turtles. Yet he records without comment his own delight in turtle meat and soup, made from creatures he had killed, and describes the "extreme tameness" of the birds, which allowed him to approach near enough to "kill them with a switch" or knock them down "with a cap or hat." He habitually killed and opened up the stomachs of creatures to discover what they ate. But that was "science." Killing for other purposes was "cruelty."

If Darwin was ambivalent about the fact of cruelty, he was also confused about its motivation. How could impersonal nature be, as he said, "horribly cruel"? Judgments of value about nature's actions, design, efficiency, and success or failure often slipped into his narratives. He found it no easier than anyone else to imagine an existence without object, where, in Thomas Hobbes's bleak phrase, "there is no contentment but in proceeding." So while surrendering gradually any belief in any kind of omnipotent being or any conceivable afterlife, he continued to believe, or half-believe, in nature as a success story, an endless ascent to higher organisms, more efficient, more adaptable, more capable of coping with their surroundings.

But was that where his theory of natural selection actually led? It was clearly one of the most powerful and inclusive ideas ever produced by man. While Darwin was still alive, in 1880,

Leslie Stephen, in an article in the *Fortnightly Review* called "An Attempted Philosophy of History," predicted that the new science of life would conquer all: "Darwinism has acted like a charm, affecting the whole development of modern thought . . . we classify the ablest thinkers by the relation which their opinions bear to it, and whatever its ultimate fate, no one can doubt that it will be the most conspicuous factor in modern speculation." Stephen, the polymath creator of the *Dictionary of National Biography*, was an updated version of Herbert Spencer and a progenitor of the Bloomsbury Group. His prediction has proved broadly correct, even though for a time it looked as though the ideas of Marx or Freud or Einstein might prove more powerful and durable.

There was, it is true, a moment early in the twentieth century when it seemed possible that Darwinism might be toppled. As Mendel and his theory of genetics were rediscovered, spread rapidly, and were accepted and enlarged upon, some thought genetics was incompatible with Darwin. But after the First World War, Ronald Fisher showed that it was possible to reconcile Darwin and Mendel. Indeed, said Fisher, "Mendelism supplied the missing parts of the structure erected by Darwin." Darwin showed the *what* of evolution and the *why*, natural selection. Now Mendel had produced the *how*, genetics. This was reinforced when Hermann Joseph Muller showed that genes are artificially mutable. Thanks to Fisher and Muller and others, such as J. B. S. Haldane, by the 1930s, Darwin-Mendelism was triumphant. The way was then open for James Watson and Francis Crick to discover the double helix structure of DNA. So on to the genome and the present infinite possibilities of the science.

But if Darwin's natural selection survived to become an essential part of modern genetics, it also acquired an intellectual life of its own. First was its new universality. It was seen that natural selection applied not merely to organic nature—the entire range of species from vegetation to man—but to the inanimate world as well. Natural selection had to be seen as a destructive force as well as a productive one. The survivals are what remain after nature has swept away the rest as rubbish. This applies equally to everything in the universe, from galaxies down to suns and planets, then with planets to tectonic plates and continents. A typical case is a mountain. It exists because nothing, as yet, has come along to destroy it. One of weaker composition and construction would have been reduced to sand and rubble and absorbed in the soil.

Although the process whereby durable mountains are sorted out from broken ones may be physically different from the sorting out of vegetable and organic matter, both are part of selection by nature. Once this is grasped, it is hard to see any moral purpose in nature or indeed any purpose at all. We come under exactly the same fundamental rules as a piece of rock. Nature grinds on but without object or purpose or rationale, long- or short-term. There is no point whatsoever in existence. Nonexistence is just as significant. Or rather, nothing whatsoever signifies. The result is nihilism.

It is hard to believe that Darwin himself would have accepted this huge, bottomless emptiness of life. Or rather, perhaps because he felt it yawning, he averted his eyes from the big issues and focused them on the small: climbing plants, orchids, insectivorous plants, worms. The truth is, long before he died, he had lost control over his own theory. It was taking him where he did not wish to go. The point at which he lost control can be precisely identified. It was when he decided that natural selection, to be internally coherent, has to be comprehensive and universal. But if this is so, there is no essential difference between man and any other animal. The differences, however obvious and seemingly enormous, are of degree, not of kind. Darwin was sure this was and is so, and therefore, having written *Origin*, he wrote *Descent* and *Expressions*, whose prime object is to prove it. And then, having proved it, he averted his eyes from the consequence—the colossal vacuum that swallows the universe in pointlessness.

However, Darwin, by not thinking the thing through, missed a very important paradox. It can more easily be grasped if we see natural selection as destructive as well as constructive—and not only destructive but self-destructive. Once natural selection had created man, it was in its own danger zone. Human beings think. Well, so evidently do many other creatures, even worms, as Darwin showed. Human beings are conscious, and self-conscious. Well, so perhaps are some other beings, though we cannot be sure. What we can be reasonably sure about is that no other animal except man is self-conscious to the point of examining the nature of existence, the point of it or its pointlessness, and then seeking ways of doing something about it.

It is at this stage in evolution that natural selection falters and ceases to work with all its previous triumphalism and certitude. We speak of "man taming nature"—Darwin used the phrase himself. What he did not foresee was man taming natural selection.

Yet it was already happening in his lifetime. He could see dim implications. He opposed birth control because it threatened the "geometrical progression" by which (he thought) human beings reproduced themselves. He opposed vaccination because it hindered nature's ability to destroy the weak and select the strong. What he did not live to see was an age in which mankind would use its ever growing intellectual, physical, and indeed spiritual resources to frustrate natural selection at almost every point of its operations. So anxious was Darwin to prove that natural selection had produced humanity that he was blind to the fact that it was also producing humanitarianism, a moral force that made the operation of natural selection ultimately far more difficult, if not impossible.

Looking to the future, there seemed no end to the way in which the development of humanity, originally by natural selection at its most spectacular, should work to frustrate its destructive and unpitying logic. In the fifteenth century, European populations, having recovered from the Black Death, were expanding rapidly and suffering from land hunger. By their ingenuity in constructing oceangoing vessels and maps and navigational instruments, they were enabled to move overseas and begin the process of conquering and occupying the territories of weaker peoples, exterminating or enslaving them. With nature operating throughout the universe in its process of destroying the weaker and selecting the stronger, the earth itself is ultimately threatened with annihilation, and all its inhabitants. Long before that time, however, the likelihood is that humanity will have mastered long-distance travel in the universe, seeking out and occupying inhabitable areas as our fifteenth-century predecessors did in the Americas.

None of this, of course, invalidates the principle of selecting the fittest, which Darwin identified as the way nature operates. Indeed the fact that the superintelligent animal, *Homo sapiens*, which nature created by selection, has progressed to frustrating, at many points, the process that made us so formidable, is itself a further demonstration of its truth. So Darwin's theory remains one of the great scientific explanations of all time, and its confirmation and blending with Mendelism, which supplied its missing dimension, has produced the science of genetics, moving at accelerating speed to illuminate the mysteries of life. Darwin is here to stay among the select band of leaders who dispersed the darkness of ignorance.

However, none of this justifies the enthusiasm of the Darwinian fundamentalists, who over the last few decades have sought to give Darwin a quasi-divine status and to abuse those who subject him and his work to the continuing critical scrutiny that is the essence of true science. Darwin was the first to admit his limitations, and as this little book has shown, they were numerous and sometimes important. Darwin clung to, for instance, the teaching of Lamarck, that acquired characteristics could be inherited, and this led him into absurdities. Post-Mendelian genetics has shown that Lamarck and Darwin were wrong on this point.

What is particularly unfortunate is that the biologists responsible for Darwinian fundamentalism have themselves been deified by an ingenious but perverse band of philosophers, who have acted rather like the slave-ants that Darwin studied, in subjecting their own professional interests to the demands of their biological masters. This alliance of overexuberant science with bad philosophy is a formidable obstacle to truth and the expansion of knowledge.

That knowledge will expand we can be certain, and at an accelerating pace and in directions we cannot possibly predict. This book is written from the viewpoint of a historian, and while all theories of history are vainglorious absurdities, doomed to eventual oblivion, history does teach certain lessons, one of which is that science, like everything else, becomes out of date. And another is that nature is full of surprises. After a lifetime of scientific research, J. B. S. Haldane ruefully concluded, "The universe is not only queerer than we suppose, but queerer than we *can* suppose." It is a sobering but also an intoxicating thought that we are just at the beginning of the process of acquiring knowledge. How Darwin would have agreed!

Further Reading

THERE ARE NOW countless books about Darwin, but it is essential to read what he actually wrote. Of his more important books, there is a good edition of *The Voyage of the Beagle* (as it is now called) in the Wordsworth Classics of World Literature, with an introduction by David Amigoni. Penguin Classics publishes *The Origin of Species,* with an introduction by John Wyon Burrow. Gibson Square Books publishes *The Descent of Man,* with an introduction by Richard Dawkins. *The Expression of the Emotions in Men and Animals* is published by Penguin with an introduction by Joe Cain. The Oxford University Press has published a useful edition titled *Darwin's Evolutionary Writings,* including the autobiographical material in an introduction by James A. Secord. All these are in paperback. *Charles Darwin's Shorter Publications,* edited by John Van Wyhe, is published by Cambridge University Press (2009). There is a complete edition, *The Works of Charles Darwin,* in 29 volumes, edited by Paul H. Barrett and R. B. Freeman (London 1986). *The Correspondence of Charles Darwin,* edited by Frederick Burkhardt et al., is published by Cambridge University Press, in 18 volumes and continuing (1985–). Also useful is

The Cambridge Companion to "The Origin of Species", edited by Michael Ruse and Robert J. Richards (2009).

The official biography of Darwin by his son Francis is still worth reading and is epitomized in the old *Dictionary of National Biography*. Among modern biographies, there are Janet Browne, *Charles Darwin*, 2 vols. (London 1995–2002); and Adrian Desmond and James Moore, *Darwin* (London 1991). For his wife, see James D. Loy and Kent M. Loy, *Emma Darwin: A Victorian Life* (University Press of Florida 2010). For Darwin and slavery, see Adrian Desmond and James Moore, *Darwin's Sacred Cause* (Penguin 2010). For the historical background, see chapter 13, "The Evolutionary Moment," in K. Theodore Hoppen, *The Mid-Victorian Generation, England 1846–1886* (Oxford University Press 1998). For post-Darwin developments, see Matt Ridley, *Genome* (London 1999).

Index